MW01267882

So What Do I Do About Me?

So What Do I Do About Me?

Surviving the In-Between Years

Kirk Hill

1993
TEACHER IDEAS PRESS
A Division of
Libraries Unlimited, Inc.
Englewood, Colorado

Dedicated to
Jeran Artery, who remembers how it feels to be fourteen,
and to
Bret Bowden Hill, who cares about people's feelings.

Copyright © 1993 Margaret O. Hill
All Rights Reserved
Printed in the United States of America

No part of this publication may be reproduced, stored in a retrieval system, or transmitted, in any form or by any means, electronic, mechanical, photocopying, recording, or otherwise, without the prior written permission of the publisher. An exception is made for individual library media specialists and teachers who may make copies of activity sheets or poster pages for classroom use in a single school.

TEACHER IDEAS PRESS
A Division of
Libraries Unlimited, Inc.
P.O. Box 6633
Englewood, CO 80155-6633

This book is a work of fiction. The characters, names, incidents, and dialogue are products of the author's imagination. Any resemblance to actual persons or events is purely coincidental.

Library of Congress Cataloging-in-Publication Data

Hill, Kirk.
    So what do I do about me? : surviving the in-between years / Kirk Hill.
    xxiii, 136 p. 17x25 cm.
    Includes index.
    ISBN 1-56308-048-6
    1. Psychology--Study and teaching (Secondary) 2. Human behavior--Study and teaching (Secondary) 3. Adolescent psychology--Study and teaching (Secondary) 4. Middle school students--Psychology--Study and teaching (Secondary) 5. Middle schools--Curricula. I. Title.
BF77.H55   1993
155.5--dc20   93-523
                                                       CIP

Contents

Sets theme of book, which is: You can't do much to change the world, but you do have control over your own life. Introduces author, Kirk, and Human Behavior class at middle school. How book came to be written and what the process will be.

Difference between *who I am* and *how I am*. Having control over your life without hurting yourself or others. How does it feel to be a teacher?

How can you be yourself with all those people out there telling you who to be? How feelings influence the way you act. Choosing the appropriate roles for different situations.

Deciding who you are. How to be yourself and still accept the role of son or daughter. Adopting the philosophy of "I count, you count."

You didn't choose to be exactly the way you are. You are made up of pieces of all those ancestors in your background — plus everything that has happened to you from the moment you were conceived in the shelter of your mother's body. No wonder people have trouble understanding you, and no wonder *you* have trouble understanding that amazing person who is you.

Talk about making a fool of yourself! Happens all the time. The only consolation is it happens to everyone else all the time too. You and Charlie Brown and all those other imperfect people blushing their way through life. Who is Charlie Brown? He's you.

Actions grow out of needs — physical and emotional. What happens when your needs clash with someone else's? You both cry Ouch. So then you both need salve and bandages and love and understanding.

Sometimes it seems you are always looking back over your shoulder, wishing you could live that episode over. If only you could erase some of those words. If you could only have foreseen what effect your actions would have on someone else. You may even have made a choice that permanently damaged or destroyed a life. Instead of grieving over what can't be changed, you can keep remembering that wisdom grows out of mistakes. There are all those next times ahead of you. Think ahead rather than back.

What do you see in him or her — that someone who is so different from you? Maybe that person represents one of your secret longings to be someone you aren't. So what is the attraction? Is it a healthy one for you? What might the consequences of your relationship be? Can you keep on being you and at the same time accept that other person the way he or she is without getting hurt in the process?

What does it take to turn a dream of an evening into a nightmare? Our country's number one drug maybe? How would you have handled the scene?

Three million what? Could you or your best friend be one of that three million?

Mad at someone? Sure. Who isn't? Just be sure what you say and do doesn't hit the wrong targets.

There's a need for separating personal problems into two categories: those that are the result of circumstance and those that individuals create for themselves. Who's to blame for your problems? Not you surely!

Feel like crying? So cry. Especially if a loved one dies. When that occurs, there may be a layer of guilt for you to deal with on top of the sorrow.

How do you cope with a life you didn't order? So you have problems. You always have, and you always will. At least you have company — everyone!

Your world is different from the one your parents knew at this age. No wonder they're worried. Their parents were worried too. And someday you will be if you have children. What are your attitudes about sexual activity in today's society, especially among children and teenagers?

Spoken words are simply pieces of language. What causes them to spring to life and to take on different meanings? Your tone of voice and the body language that accompanies that voice. What you say isn't necessarily what the listener hears.

Who owns you? Your parents or foster parents? Other adults in your life? The law? Your friends? The gang? Your enemies? Your boss? In the long run, only you. Those other people in your life have immense influence on your thoughts, your beliefs, and your behavior. But only you are completely responsible for you.

That new boy or girl in your life! Up until now you've been aware of the condition of being in love. Now suddenly....

So it's dating time in your life. Big deal! Knowing how to act in a relationship should come naturally. Should be a cinch. It's not. If only you could play that scene over.

Who are the "losers" in your school? How did they get that way? What do you do about them? Nothing? Something? It all depends.

You may not always look forward to going home. You may not be happy — or in some cases even safe — when you're there. But what would it feel like if home just weren't?

Your own home may look pretty good after all. Chances are you will never hear the words *Time's up; you gotta move right away.*

When you see a movie or read a good story, you may have the magical feeling that you actually are one of the characters on the screen or between the covers of that book. So what about the people around you? How would it feel to dwell in someone else's skin?

Ever feel like running away from life but there's nowhere to go? We all do some running away—sometimes healthful, sometimes not. You might lose yourself in a good story or a glowing daydream. You could get an illness brought on by emotional distress. You may try to ease your hurting by using alcohol or other drugs. You could leave home. You could refuse to deal with your problems. When and how do *you* bug out? Which are harmless escapes? Which cause problems in addition to the ones you have already?

At best, life plays tricks on us. One writer said, "Reality is what happens when you had something else in mind." Many painful happenings can be prevented, though, if you train yourself to weigh your actions ahead of time.

Have you been wondering, along with Kirk, what happened to homeless Danfra and Aaron? Kirk once said, "Kids do grow up." What about Danny and Aaron? Will they "grow up" or remain society's "children" forever?

Do you always have to "act your age"? Let's assume that in each of us there are three beings: child, parent, and adult. Is it okay for adults to act like children sometimes? Are there times when it's appropriate for you to play the role of parent to your parents or to someone else? In some cases, could problems among families and other groups be solved more successfully if all the members acted like adults?

Not just children need parents. Everyone does at some time or other. Being grown-up and wise doesn't mean you don't need other people to help you over some rocky spots. Who are the "parents" in your life besides Mom or Dad?

So you're not a carbon copy of your parents and other adults anymore. You're drifting off in a new direction. The people who love you and worry about you keep calling you back to see things as they do. How can you live with the differences without hurting you and others? Maybe you can't always. Most of the time, though?

Take another look at those adult values that are wished on you. Could it be that you and that other generation aren't so far apart after all?

Are you prejudiced? Of course not. But look again. Do others see you as biased in your views? Are you hurting because of someone's unreasonable feelings about you? How can you preserve the right to feel any way you want to without hurting others?

Why do people keep saying stuff that cuts you down, makes you squirm, pounds away at your self-confidence? Just think what they might say if they appreciated what a great kid you really are.

Oh, but maybe you're guilty too. Which side of the other person do you see and criticize? What might you have said to build up someone else? It's not too late, you know.

Does honesty mean tramping on other people's feelings? How can you tell how *you* feel without damaging how that other person feels?

Can you express your disappointment in someone else without damaging him or her? Absolutely. It's all in the words you choose and the love you wrap them in.

So now Kirk has written a book, and he's a reformed character? Well, no. We couldn't stand him if he were perfect. Little danger of that! Kirk is still Kirk, still fretting about the world. But the book tells us he has done considerable growing and changing. That's the task for each of you: Keep being yourself, but continue to improve yourself as your life moves forward.

Acknowledgments

Special thanks to the following for their editorial help and encouragement:

Jeran Artery for editorial assistance.

Ms. Dean Brooks and her REACH class at Conrad Ball Middle School, Loveland, Colorado, who used portions of this book and gave useful suggestions for its improvement.

Ms. Julie Goettsch, principal, Conrad Ball Middle School, for her enthusiasm and encouragement.

Teen editors Melanie Mielke, Jill Kelley, and Josh Barchers for their up-to-date suggestions.

And especially to editor Suzanne Barchers of Teacher Ideas Press, a division of Libraries Unlimited.

Introduction

At all ages our first interest and concern is self. Early in life we begin to ask ourselves, Who exactly am I? Why do I act the way I do, and why do others behave as they do?

In order to do a graceful job of living, we need to understand feelings and behavioral motivation. For instance, the way you act in a situation elicits certain reactions from others. Those reactions awaken an emotional response in you. That emotion (or group of emotions) dictates your next behavior, which, in turn, elicits further feedback from others. Thus, feelings and behavior are so interrelated as to have the power to create problems—and to resolve them.

Psychology is one of the most popular high-school courses in our country's curriculum; however, as one fifteen-year-old pointed out, it's between ages twelve and fifteen that students would most welcome classes in human behavior—a course not offered in most elementary, junior-high, and middle schools, whose student population includes the in-betweens (no longer children, yet not quite young adults).

The Task Force of the Carnegie Council on Adolescent Development has prepared a report on the education of young adolescents. The document, *Turning Points, Preparing American Youth for the 21st Century*, states that, "For many youth 10 to 15 years old, early adolescence offers opportunities to choose a path toward a productive and fulfilling life. For many others, it represents their last chance to avoid a diminished future." The report says further, "Middle grade schools—junior high, intermediate, or middle schools—are potentially society's most powerful force to recapture millions of youth adrift" (8).

The task force also makes the accusation that "[p]hysical and mental health dimensions of educating the young adolescent, dimensions so vital to the ancient Greeks, are largely lost on us Americans." The report adds, "Mild to severe mental health problems are widespread among young adolescents" (60, 61).

Logically, might not mental health be improved by emphasizing self-understanding and by learning to grapple with the everyday problems that are characteristic of each age group—in short, the art of simply learning how to live?

The overall philosophy of the Task Force of the Carnegie Council is about the education of the whole child, encompassing academic proficiency, living skills, and mental and emotional health. That implies a deep understanding of *human behavior*—what one teacher refers to as "the how comes and the outcomes."

The task force emphasizes that "all too often" the curriculum of the middle-grade school is not compatible with the intellectual and emotional needs of preadolescents and young adolescents.

This shortcoming suggests that courses in human development and behavior might deserve a greater share of the curriculum. Currently, personal problems and relationships are handled in connection with home economics, social studies, and health classes. But whether offered as a course in itself or included in more traditional classes, an organized presentation of the various aspects of human behavior should not be delayed until senior-high school.

Because flexibility is the hallmark of the ideal middle school, the study of human beings should be a natural inclusion for that age group.

Asked what kind of book he would like at the middle-school level, a fourteen-year-old specified, "Something easy to read. Not one of those big thick textbooks telling us what we ought to do." With that authoritative advice in mind, this supplementary reading volume has been prepared in the hope of fulfilling the following objectives:

1. To explore the ordinary, day-to-day kinds of problems that are common to most young adolescents, not just those at risk.

2. To strengthen self-esteem by emphasizing individuality.

3. To emphasize self-responsibility.

4. To encourage the weighing of consequences of choices.

5. To understand the whys of human behavior.

6. To underscore the universality of feelings.

7. To emphasize the importance of becoming a good parent to oneself.

8. To suggest ways of establishing improved relationships, especially with family members, peers, employers, teachers, and other educators.

9. To encourage students to interact among themselves in a caring way.

10. To encourage students to view parents, teachers, and counselors as human beings who can be supportive and enjoyable to know.

11. To build a philosophy based on the needs of self and others.

12. To regulate behavior based on the concept of "I count, you count."

Instruction concerning ordinary, everyday problems in living is prerequisite to inoculating youngsters against the major pitfalls that threaten the many millions of adolescents who are at a high risk of school failure, destructive behavior, or both. How can a young person be persuaded to resist gang activity before he or she has learned how to parent himself or herself? Who can face the toughness of life before becoming the master of his or her emotions? Who can deal with a major problem such as drug involvement before first learning ways of managing the routine problems of home, classroom, and workplace?

Those same children who needed reading readiness at age five are now the adolescents who need living readiness if they are to survive in a world that needs a lot of mending.

REFERENCE

Carnegie Council on Adolescent Development. *Turning Points, Preparing American Youth for the 21st Century*. New York: Carnegie Corporation of New York, 1989.

How to Use This Book

According to John Lounsbury, former editor of *Middle School Journal*, a correlation exists between the level of pupil-teacher interaction and student self-esteem and feelings of well-being. With that in mind, this volume was prepared as a classroom tool involving teacher and students.

Ideally, the book might speak to the preteen and teenager at that awkward in-between stage of being thought of by others as still a child and by the young person himself or herself as a child no longer. It hurts to leave some of those pieces of childhood behind, and it's also uncomfortable to take on some responsibilities of growing up.

One purpose of this book is to cause the reader to identify with the characters with reactions such as: "I know just how that kid felt." "That's like something that happened to me." "I feel as if I know the characters in this book." "Maybe I'll try that; it might work for me." "I'm glad to read about someone who isn't too good to be true."

Some specific ways the book might be used include:

- As a textbook. The teacher and students could read the chapters in chronological order and carry out some or all of the activities, or make up their own follow-up activities.

- As a work read aloud and discussed in relation to the students' lives at any given time. The "Something to..." sections in the chapters can prompt discussion, reflection, class projects, and so forth.

- As extra reading in or out of class and either assigned or read voluntarily.

- As supplementary reading for units in regular classes such as science, health, home economics, or social studies.

- As part of the school library or classroom library along with self-help and self-understanding materials.

- As a tool in specially created classes for dealing with the problems of early adolescence. By way of example, a middle school in Colorado has a REACH (Reaching Every Adolescent through Caring and Helping) program. This is an adviser-advisee system in which every student is in close contact with a faculty member or another adult in the school—someone in the youngster's life who can be counted on when need arises. REACH classes meet for one period each school day. Some days are for reading, others are for discussion, writing, and other follow-up activities. Kirk's class falls in this last category. Chapters are not necessarily to be read in sequence but rather as they seem to relate to events going on in the students' lives.

This book presents a small piece of the everyday world as viewed through the eyes of fourteen-year-old Kirk Hill, a less than scholastically inclined eighth-grader disenchanted with his world, or at least with *the* world in its present state. Kirk is persuaded by Miss Hambrick, a teacher's assistant, to put his thoughts and experiences into book form on tape with the intention that such a volume might be helpful to other kids struggling with the typical problems of growing up.

Certain chapters of Kirk's book might be useful in relation to specific issues or crises as they arise. For instance:

- Self-identity: Who am I, and why am I this way? chapters 1, 2, 3, 4, 5, 18

- Feelings of inadequacy, embarrassment, damaged self-image. chapters 1, 6, 12, 13, 16, 19, 20

- Getting along with the people in your life. chapters 7, 12, 13, 17, 18, 32, 33, 34, 35, 36

- Dealing with problems. Choices: looking back and looking ahead. chapters 8, 13, 15, 16, 25, 26

- Friendships that don't run smoothly.
  chapters 9, 10, 11

- Death of a loved one.
  chapter 14

- Someone new in your life.
  chapters 10, 19, 21, 22, 23, 24, 27

- You and your parents, foster parents, or guardians.
  chapters 4, 5, 12, 13, 16, 28, 29, 30, 31, 32, 33, 34, 35, 36

- Prejudice.
  chapter 32

- Special problems (alcohol, homelessness, parents).
  chapters 8, 10, 11, 13, 14, 15, 18, 19, 21, 22, 23, 24, 25, 26, 27, 32, 33, 34, 35, 36, 37

Prologue

Each year the social studies teacher in this book, Dale Rickman, hears complaints from students about the curriculum. Too much of the subject matter seems not to meet their needs and seems irrelevant to their lives. So Mr. Rickman puts the question to them: "What kinds of subject matter do you like to study? What courses answer your needs?" He receives many of the expected answers: science experiments, music, short story, art, creative writing, science fiction, gym. One unexpected reply was "People."

So, okay, Mr. Rickman decided, Why not study people? That's the one subject we are all faced with every day, including that one puzzling person we are all stuck with for a lifetime—ourself! Accordingly, the "class about us" came into being under the name Human Behavior. It seemed only natural that the course would grow out of the students' everyday problems. The theme of the class and this book is, in Mr. Rickman's words, "You can't change the world, but you can do something about you."

1

The World's a Disaster

The world's a mess! I know that from listening to radio and TV and reading the newspapers and seeing what's going on around me. I'd know it anyway on account of the bummed-out way I feel at times. Mr. Dean, my counselor at school, says it's natural for kids to be depressed sometimes.

Anyway, I get to feeling disgusted about the mess adults have made of the world. War, people hungry and homeless, murders and gang violence, the ozone hole, overpopulation, endangered animals.

My mom says, "Kirk, someday your kids will be saying that same thing about you and your generation."

When I started fussing in Human Behavior class about the shape things are in, our teacher, Mr. Rickman, said, "You can't change the entire world, Kirk."

The trouble with complaining to adults is that they expect you to do something about your problems. Mr. Rickman said some change has to take place inside of ourselves. He also said that each of us owns a little chunk of the world, and we can do something to make that piece a better place.

I was still wondering about that when Miss Hambrick chimed in with a comment. Miss Hambrick is a teacher's aide for Mr. Rickman. She helps us with reading and subjects we have trouble with. What she said was, "Kirk, with all your whining you should write a book."

I laughed and said, "In your dreams." She and I both know I have trouble writing a paragraph.

"I mean it," she said. "Only instead of writing all of it, you could say some of it."

"Say it? You mean like talking?" I asked in a choky voice.

1

She nodded. "Talk into a tape recorder. You do a good job with talking." (Especially when I'm not supposed to, I thought.)

"So why couldn't you make a talking book?" Miss Hambrick suggested.

"What about?" I felt backed into a corner.

"The way you feel about things. Your family. Friends. Problems. Teachers. Classmates. Your after-school job. The world."

"Yeah, but I could never remember all those things. Like what people said and exactly what all happened."

Miss Hambrick patted my shoulder. "You'd just write things down or say things into the recorder the way you remember them. In fact, you could record some conversations on your own tape recorder. That's what our blind students do to help them remember what went on in classes. You like to record things."

"Well, yes. Music and stuff like that, but —"

Miss Hambrick was really getting excited about her idea by this time. She said: "Later, I could put whatever you've written, and what's on the tapes, on the computer and print it out to share with other kids. Besides, it will help you with reading. When it's printed, you can read it back easily because you'll already know what it says."

I must have looked worried because Miss Hambrick said: "Quit frowning. This is something you can do — with help, of course."

Miss Hambrick has told us a lot of times that she gets upset with people who keep saying "I can't."

She patted my arm and said, "And just think, when you've finished, you'll have a talking book other people can listen to."

I managed to quit frowning and nodded my head wimpishly.

So that's how come I have to write this book. Imagine *me* writing a book! And all because I said the world is a mess.

Since I'm going to do this, I suppose I'd better tell something about me. Like in regular books at the library where they tell something about the author.

Anyway, about this author.... To begin with I should explain some things about our school. It used to be a junior high for seventh- to ninth-graders, but now it's Fraser Kline Middle School for sixth- to eighth-graders. It's different from regular grade school where everyone is in a certain grade. Here, we are put in classes that are right for us, according to what kind of learning we need.

That's part of the reason for the Human Behavior class. At high school they have psychology classes, but we are curious about ourselves too and how come we act the way we do. The teachers here figure that learning how to live in the real world is as important as things like math, science, and English. They say doing a good job of living is something that has to be learned; it doesn't just come naturally. That's why the assignments in Human Behavior class are different and sometimes far out. Mr. Rickman says we're supposed to come out of here with some tools for survival, like getting along with the people in our lives.

Human Behavior is part of our school's Reachout program. The reason for that name is that our school philosophy is to reach out to people—not only reaching out to know and help others, but reaching out for friendship and help when we need it.

Each student is assigned to a Reachout class with a teacher who is especially close to every kid in that class. The teacher is someone we can confide in and who helps us with our problems.

According to Miss Hambrick, I will actually write parts of this book myself. My English teacher, Mrs. Atkins, will help with the spelling, punctuation, sentences, and grammar. (Important things, I guess.) Other parts of the book will be what I say into the tape recorder for Miss Hambrick to put on the computer later on.

A little more about me. I'm one of the oldest kids in the school but not one of the smartest by a couple of miles. The reason I'm one of the older fourteen-year-olds is that my birthday is in October, so I didn't make it into first grade until I was almost seven.

The kids who read this book are going to think they could write a book like this. I can tell them one thing: If *I* can, they can.

When I talk about being an author, the kids laugh. But just wait till they see the darn thing in print or hear it on tape. We'll see who's laughing then.

Something a Class Can Do

Mr. Rickman latched onto Miss Hambrick's idea right away and decided to get the whole class involved. He had us cut headlines out of newspapers about bad things going on in the world. We pinned them onto half of the bulletin board. For every bad-news headline we found a good-news one to offset it for the other half of the bulletin board.

The purpose of this is to remind us that all of life is a struggle between good and evil. Our job is to see that the good guys win as often as possible.

2

Who Am I?

You might want to do this exercise Mr. Rickman gave to our Human Behavior class. Answer the question Who are you? with the first three responses that pop into your mind:

I am_____

I am_____

I am_____

We didn't know what that was leading up to, but we went ahead anyway. We put down a lot of things like: I am bored. I am trapped. I am happy. I am sad. I am different. I am depressed. I am fed up. I am tired of being bossed around by adults.

The next day Mr. Rickman read the papers to us. He said: "I didn't ask *how* you are; I asked *who* you are. There were only a few answers to that. For instance: I am Lance Mowbry. I am a Hispanic. I am a student. I am my dog's master."

We laughed when Mr. Rickman read that answer about being "my dog's master." The teacher said it wasn't all that funny. He said the person who wrote that is probably saying other people have too much control over him. Then he went on with a big lecture about how you need to feel in control of your own life.

Mr. Rickman gave some examples of what people do when they think they are losing control of their lives. For example, the kids start jerking around in class, and the teacher figures maybe she can't get their attention. She starts yelling at one girl — probably one who bugs her most of the time. She sends the girl out of class and tells her not to come back. That isn't a good idea, because the principal says the girl has to stay in that class. So then the girl and the teacher are stuck with each other.

Another example would be the dad who is afraid he is losing control of his teenage son, so he decides to show him who's boss. He tells his kid to shape up or get out. The father probably doesn't mean it, but the son moves out. He finds he can't make a living and gets in trouble — ends up in jail maybe. Then the parents panic and make their kid move back home.

Mr. Rickman says hijackers and arsonists and many other bad guys often feel they have never had control over their own lives. The bad things they do are their way of trying to control other people.

Mr. Rickman says when we are parents to be sure to help our children to learn how to have some control over their own lives without hurting themselves or other people. I wonder how you go about doing that. It must be rough to be a parent. Or a teacher. I never gave that much thought before. It's not just kids who have problems, I guess.

In the example about the students messing around, the teacher is worried that the class is getting out of hand. Mr. Rickman had us talk about it.

For instance, Was sending the girl out of class a good way of handling the problem? Why did we think it was or wasn't? If we were the teacher, how would we deal with the problem?

Of course, we had lot of ideas about that. We always know what someone else should have done. We got so carried away with that discussion that we wound up acting the situation out. Role-playing, Mr. Rickman calls it. Several of us took turns being the teacher. That was fun.

Naturally the kids who played the pupil roles had a blast giving the teacher a bad time.

Then we talked about how it felt to be the teacher. Comfortable? Uncomfortable? Embarrassing? Frightening? Angry? Nervous?

Some of the kids who played the teacher role came up with good ideas. For instance, Nedra started writing on the board. We were curious, so we settled down long enough to read what she wrote. What it said was:

Brothers and sisters have I none. This man's father is my father's son. Who is this man?

The class was looking blank by that time, but you could tell some of us were trying to figure out the answer.

Nedra said, "Sharpen your little minds on that while I get out my grade book and see who might come up with an *A*."

At the end of the period, some of us were still trying to figure out who "this man" was.

Nedra got her idea from Mrs. Atkins, our English teacher. When we come into her class, we have to pick up a slip of paper that has a puzzle on it. She gives us a grade on how we work at it. Mrs. Atkins gives grades for what she calls "on-the-job" skills.

We complained that only the smart kids could figure out the puzzles. She said, "Not everyone can do the brainteaser, but smart or not, a person can get to work on time."

When we got through with our teacher-pupil role-playing in Mr. Rickman's class, he said: "In your next class try to imagine how the teacher is feeling. Tomorrow we'll talk about ways we could help a teacher to feel good about his or her class."

Just before the bell rang, Mr. Rickman laid something else on us. He said: "By the way, here's a trade secret. If you want to have people like you, do things to make them feel good about themselves."

3

Well Then, Who Am I Really?

So Mr. Rickman says most of the things we wrote on the completion exercise didn't answer the question *Who are you?*

We asked him how do we know who we are.

He said: "You complain because people won't let you just be yourselves. But how can you be yourself if you don't know who 'yourself' is?"

"How do we find out?" we asked.

"Take you, for instance, Rusty," Mr. R. said.

(I'll call Mr. Rickman "Mr. R." most of the time from now on, since I use his name so often in this book.)

Rusty was dozing off, but he came to life in a hurry when Margarita Flores punched him.

"Huh?" he said.

"Who exactly are you, Rusty?" Mr. R. asked.

Rusty looked dazed. "Who?" he repeated.

Mr. R. nodded.

"Well, uh...." Rusty began.

Mr. R. said, "Let me answer for you, since the bell is bound to ring before you get it figured out."

That would sound like a put-down if it were any other teacher, but we know Mr. Rickman cares about us, so he can get away with being sarcastic when he's trying to get something important across.

Rusty sat up straight and closed his mouth.

Mr. R. said, "Suppose I said you were a bored eighth-grader who wants a graduation diploma but who doesn't want to work for it."

"Well, no, not really!" Rusty said in a loud, nervous voice.

"Oh, so you *don't* want a diploma?"

7

"Oh, but I *do*! That is.... I mean...." Rusty was getting flustered.

Mr. Rickman put his hand on Rusty's shoulder. "Relax," he said. "I put you on the spot like this to make a point."

We looked at him, wondering what the point was. He told us what it was. "Rusty, at this moment you aren't the same person you were a few minutes ago. Right now you are a scared, embarrassed little kid. Correct?"

Rusty said: "Embarrassed anyway. *Not* a little kid, though."

"A little kid for the moment," Mr. R. insisted, "because I treated you like one by making you feel foolish in front of the class. I was playing the part of a teacher coming on heavy, so that made you feel like a child."

Rusty said: "I catch your drift. People act different ways at different times."

"Right," Mr. R. agreed. "I'm not in the habit of making my students feel childish. I must admit, though, I'm a bit sensitive about people who sleep through my fascinating classes."

Everyone laughed. We know a teacher's joke when we hear one.

"What an alert class," Mr. Rickman said.

Somehow he always manages to stay in control, even while he lets us feel as if we are. I guess that's what being a good teacher or a good parent is: being in control and letting kids feel in control at the same time.

We spent some time talking about the degrading times when we felt we were being treated like children instead of the age we are. We answered questions like: How did it make you feel? What did you say or do? What had you said or done in the first place to cause someone to treat you like a child?

Janelle mentioned that there are also times when we are expected to act older than we are. Like Lance saying he is expected to be the husband and father in the family since his parents got a divorce.

Marcie told us she feels more like her mom's sister than her daughter on account of her mother confiding in her so much. "It gets embarrassing sometimes," Marcie said. "There are some things I'd rather not know."

Mr. Rickman explained that each of us is many different people, depending on what the situation is. In a way, we are all actors, playing many different roles. We must be careful to choose which person to be at different times, in different places, and with different people.

Otherwise, we run into problems. For instance, a student who cusses in the classroom will probably find out in a hurry that those words weren't a good choice. Most teenagers know not to wear their grubbies when applying for a job. Rusty discovered that sleeping during classes doesn't go over too great.

In Mr. Rickman's class, we know when it's important to listen to the teacher and when it's all right to goof off a little. Mr. R. believes in treating us like intelligent, sensible people, but he sometimes steps out of that role in order to get our attention.

After the scene with Rusty, Mr. R. said, "Sometimes we ask for trouble because we think we can't be ourselves unless we act the same way all the time."

"But it's not being honest to pretend," Evan said.

Mr. R. told him: "It's not pretending; it's bending. It's molding yourself into a shape that fits comfortably into the situation. It's still you; it's just a different part of you. Remember, sometimes you show an ugly self to the world. That's part of who you are, but it's not your all-time self."

The teacher ended the class by reading an open letter that had appeared in a newspaper and was addressed to young people:

Dear Young Person:

I hired a teenager today, but it wasn't you. Why? Well, it wasn't entirely your not having taken the trouble to comb your hair and put on a clean shirt and jeans. That was part of it, I'll admit, but mostly it was something we refer to as "attitude." Why did you want the job? Because you were behind on your car payments, you said. So what's wrong with that? Nothing, really. It's just that the kid who got the job had taken the trouble to find out some things about our company. He talked as if he wants to get ahead—to be part of our operation, not just a wage earner. Sounds like brownie points, does it? Well, whatever it was, it worked. I decided we needed that particular person. But back to the matter of your attitude. Attitudes say something that goes beyond words. Yours seemed to say, "Take me as I am, because I'm not about to change for anyone." Just a word of advice: Next time you ask for a job, give the employer the feeling that he matters too.

When he finished reading the letter, Mr. R. told the class: "The lesson from that is that you can be yourself without always being your *same* self. Take me, for instance. I don't dress the same when I'm best man at a wedding as when I'm in the classroom. When I'm playing pool with the guys, I don't use the same kind of language as when I'm visiting with your parents. In short, I'm several people: father, husband, brother, teacher, son, neighbor, employee, guitar player. All of those people and others are me."

"I just thought of something that happened to me," I said.

"Would you like to share it?" Mr. R. suggested.

I wished right away I hadn't opened my fat mouth, but I coughed and cleared my throat a few times and finally forced some words out. "The other day when I came home from school, Mom and a bunch of her women friends were sitting around gossiping. I stopped by the table and grabbed a handful of cheese crackers. Then I told Mom I needed a permission slip to go on a field trip. She got this furious look on her face and said, 'Kirk, are you aware that I am entertaining some ladies'?"

"Well, ex-cuse me," I said. "Only it didn't sound like I was apologizing. It was more like I was being sarcastic. Later on Mom really came down on me. 'I was just being myself,' I told her."

She said, "Well, do me a favor and be someone else for a change."

Something to Write About

Mr. R. said, "Kirk's story gives me an idea for an assignment that can earn you a grade without too much pain."

I didn't look around to see if the kids were glaring at me for giving the teacher an idea for a written assignment.

The assignment was: Write a few paragraphs about an incident when you were trying to be yourself and the result was uncomfortable for you or for someone else.

Because teachers seem to get carried away with their ideas, there was more to the assignment: List the different people you are at different times. Which of these roles do you like best? Which are difficult or unpleasant for you?

Pretend you are the owner of a restaurant. You are eager to hire some teenagers. You will interview many people, but there won't be enough jobs to go around. You will have to choose from the many applicants. Make a list of qualities you will look for in order to get the best help possible.

Class members may take turns playing the roles of restaurant owner and applicants for the job. Help one another by telling why you would or would not hire certain students. This can be good practice when you are actually being interviewed for a job.

We were finally rescued by the bell. Mr. R. said: "Don't be too downcast that we didn't have time for the whole assignment. There's always tomorrow. Meantime, have fun, but not too much!"

4

Me: Self or Shadow?

We talk in Human Behavior class about finding ourselves, figuring out who we are. Mr. Rickman calls it "shaping identity." We decided that while we're real little we're sort of carbon copies of our parents. Then when we get to be teenagers, we get scared we are nothing but shadows of our parents. That's why we start doing things *our* way instead of *their* way. So then the parents get scared they're losing their little darling, and things get pretty tense.

Mr. R. says we're awkward about handling human relationships at this age, and that's because we haven't learned how yet.

He kept mentioning the letter written by that employer. He said, "To me, the most important thing in that letter is the part about giving the prospective employer the feeling that he matters too." Mr. R. said while we're trying to figure out who we are, it will help if we think in terms of "I count, and you count too." Then he went on to explain there are four philosophies in dealing with another person. *Philosophy* is what a person believes. It's a way of thinking about something.

Those philosophies about dealing with people are:

1. I count; you don't.

2. You count; I don't.

3. You don't count, and neither do I.

4. You do count, and so do I.

Our homework was to think of an example of each one. I'm not usually excited when it comes to homework, but this assignment turned me on. The examples I came up with were:

I count; you don't. There's this girl who skips school on test days. That way she has extra time to study, and besides she gets some of the answers from kids who already took the test. All she cares about is getting good grades. She doesn't care if teachers have to arrange other times for her to take the tests or that other kids get lower grades than she does.

You count; I don't. There's this mother who always slaves for her kids and doesn't expect anything out of them. The martyr type. A real pain!

I don't count; you don't count. Like when you get hung up on dope. You hurt yourself and other people who care about you. A no-win situation.

I count; you count. I couldn't think of any good example for that last one. Mr. R. said the examples I had were good, but why didn't I finish the assignment? I said every situation I thought of turned out to be I count, you don't. Somebody's always trying to win.

He said that's because people aren't very good at giving in because of everybody wanting his or her own way. The I-want-what-I-want-when-I-want-it attitude, he calls it. Everybody's too bent on filling his or her own needs to consider the other guy.

Needs have something to do with who we are, Mr. Rickman says. One of a teenager's needs is to be different from the parents. One of the parents' needs is to have the child be like them. Now how are you supposed to deal with something like that? We decided it means parents have to give in some, even though they'd rather not, and kids have to give in some, even though *they'd* rather not. Wow! I don't think my parents are going to be hip on that.

Who am I? I'm me, with my own thoughts, my own ideas, my own beliefs, my own language, my own clothes, my own private world where no one else can follow. But then, I guess I'm a piece of my parents too. The same and different all at once. Maybe that's an example of I count, and so do you.

Something to Decide

Mr. R. asked us which of the four philosophies is being used in each of these cases:

1. Mr. Rivers is determined that his son, Irvin, is going to college to become an electrical engineer. Irvin likes to work with cars and motorcycles. He wants to go to automotive school and become a first-rate mechanic. His father's answer to that is: "You have too much going for you to go to a trade school. The men in our family have college degrees, and that's my dream for you."

   Which philosophy does Mr. Rivers express in this case?

2. Della Bowers is to be married soon. She and her husband would like to live by themselves, but Della's mother wants them to live in her basement apartment. Della finally decides to go along with her mother's wishes.

   Which philosophy is Della following?

3. Angela Montez has a job checking groceries at a supermarket. Her husband feels she should give up her job to be at home with the children when they come from school. Angela insists they need the extra money her job earns. Also, she likes being away from the house some of the time. However, she wants to please her husband, and she agrees she should spend more time with the children. She finally gets a job as an aide at a nursery school, where she can work from nine in the morning until three in the afternoon.

   What is Angela's philosophy?

4. Mr. Smith is an alcoholic. When he is drunk, he abuses his wife and children. He arrives at his job late and is careless about his work. He is often absent from work due to his drinking. His doctor warns him he is destroying his health. His boss tells him that if he continues to drink, he will lose his job. His wife says she will leave him unless he agrees to go into a treatment program for alcoholism. His children stay away from home as much as possible rather than put up with his mistreatment. Mr. Smith refuses to get help for his problem.

   What philosophy is he following?

Our class talked about which case we think is being handled in the best way and why we think so.

Something to Talk About

The kids in our class were so interested in this lesson that we decided to talk about it in connection with ourselves. For instance, we told about incidents in our own lives that are examples of the four philosophies.

What happened between the people in these cases? Which ones turned out badly? Which turned out the best?

5

How Did I Get the Way I Am?

My parents and I tease each other about me being "the product of my heredity and my environment."

I asked Mrs. Atkins, my English teacher, what that means. She says *heredity* is all the traits we are born with, like eye and skin color, tallness — a lot of the things that have to do with how we look.

Heredity also has a lot to do with what we can do and how we learn. For instance, schoolwork is easier for some kids than others. Some people are good at math or spelling. I'm not one of them. School stuff comes hard for me, but I'm good at sports like swimming and running, and I'm getting pretty sharp on the computer.

Mrs. Atkins says babies aren't born knowing how to do much, but as we grow, we learn new things all the time. Some things are easy to learn for some people and hard for others. That means we have to spend more time and work harder on the things that don't come easy.

Most people think of *environment* as the world around us: trees, earth, sky, the houses we live in, and stuff like that. Our surroundings, in other words. But according to our science textbook, environment also means everything that happens to us from the minute we're born.

Even before that. While we're being carried inside of our mother's body, we are being affected by what she eats and how she takes care of her health. Like, for instance, a baby born to a mother who smokes is likely to be smaller than if the mother didn't smoke while she was pregnant. If a woman uses some drug like crack during pregnancy, her baby could be born addicted to that drug. It's all pretty scary to think of not having any control over the first nine months of our lives.

15

Anyway, we learned that each one of us is made up of a lot of traits that are passed down to us from parents, grandparents, aunts, uncles, and all those other people who have been part of our family for years back. We call those people who were part of our family "ancestors." When people talk about "family tree," they mean all the ancestors and living relatives belonging to one family. (By the way, I'm glad I didn't get my Aunt Bertha's big nose.)

Our science teacher says our heredity is like a fence around us. It lets us go a long ways in many directions, but there are some boundaries we can't cross. For instance, heredity puts a limit on how tall a person can get. Suppose it's five feet, ten inches. That's already decided by traits we got from our ancestors. Now suppose this person's mother ate properly before the baby was born. Then suppose the person grew up eating the right food and being healthy. He or she could finally reach that height of five feet, ten inches but couldn't go beyond that.

So heredity says stop when we reach limits. If I worked hard enough at it, I might become a champion swimmer, but I'd never make a doctor because I can't learn easily enough to get through all those years of college.

So my heredity says there are some things I can be and can do and other things I can't. My mom says the old saying that "anyone can do anything" isn't true, and it's important to know our limits.

In school we drew family trees showing who we might have got some of our physical traits from. When mine was finished, I knew one of my limitations: I'm a lousy artist.

What would your family tree look like if you could trace back some of your looks to the people they might have come from?

So much for looks! now what about my environment? So I'm not a brain, and I wasn't born with any big talents like music or art. Besides that, I tend to have an explosive temper. So that does it! I'm just a plain old person. I'll never do anything great, and I'll probably go right on making people mad at me by blowing up when I get mad.

Something to Remember

Our counselor, Mr. Dean, insists that no one is "just a plain old person." We are all born with a lot of good qualities that don't show up until we find them. Heredity is only a part of the picture that is you. Environment decides all the rest.

You can start with that raw material you were born with and make it into all kinds of exciting, worthwhile shapes. (Anyway, that's what Mr. Dean and the teachers keep telling us.) Me, for instance. I doubt that I could ever be an Olympic star, but I can sprint with the best members of the school track team. I probably won't go to college, but the teachers see to it that I'm learning the reading, writing, spelling, and math skills all of us need. I can also learn job skills that are just as important as college learning.

As for my temper, Mrs. Atkins says: "Kirk, don't tell me you are letting your emotions be your boss; you be the boss of them. You decide when to laugh, when to cry, when to be angry, and how to handle that anger without exploding. Pretend your feelings—your emotions—are your children. Tell them how to act so they won't get you in trouble.

"And remember, feelings are natural. It's all right to be scared, to hurt, to love and hate, to be jealous and angry and disappointed. What counts is what we do about it. Feelings are a natural part of us, but our behavior is something we learn."

I knew she was giving me a big lecture, but somehow I didn't mind too much. It's her way of telling me I'm okay.

6

The Part of Me That Is Charlie Brown

Me and Charlie Brown! Always making fools of ourselves. But of course. That's why there is a Charlie Brown. That's why someone thought him up. There's a blockhead streak in all of us. A ridiculous streak, Miss Hambrick says. (Miss Hambrick is the teacher's aide who is helping me with this book.) She calls the foolishness "a streak of Charlie Brownness."

What made me think of Charlie Brown? Well, I had to give a talk in English class. Big deal! Just get up in front of the class and tell them something, any old thing. Show-and-tell. Is that any reason to lie awake for a couple of nights? To get sick to my stomach? To make me think of dropping out of school? To decide to take a zero instead of giving the speech?

You know it!

I feel uncomfortable in that class anyway because I'm not as sharp as most of the kids in there. Some of my classes are special—they're for those of us who have trouble with regular schoolwork. But that English class is for regular kids. Mrs. Atkins makes me feel okay, though. Says I know more than I think I do. Says we are all stupid in some ways.

Anyway, that didn't make me feel better about having to give a talk in front of that bunch of brains. I even went to the school counselor about it. He said the way to get over a fear is to do what you're scared to do. He said even famous performers get nervous before they go onstage.

I left his office with my stomach still feeling like it was full of buckshot. And my knees felt like strings of cooked spaghetti.

So the next day here I am sitting through half of the English class waiting for my turn. It's like waiting for the dentist while one patient after another comes out of the office looking white and pained.

18

Finally it's my turn. I go stumbling up the aisle. I know my voice isn't going to work even if my legs do. About the time I get to the front of the room I hear this shriek: "Hey, give me back my purse!"

I look down, and here's this girl's purse hooked onto my shoe. Don't ask me how. Something like this could only happen to me. Me and Charlie Brown. Well, naturally the class cracks up. Kids are always looking for an excuse to get out of a few minutes of work.

Even if my speech had been any good, no one would have listened after that. As it was, I figured the kids were thinking how my forehead was broken out with a fresh crop of zits. Half of them fell asleep, and the others were working on homework for other classes.

Jeez, I thought! This has got to be how it feels to be a teacher when the kids don't pay attention. One thing: I'll never be good at speeches, but I'll stay awake and try to look interested next time I see that a teacher is having a bad time.

Come to think about it, that wouldn't be a bad title for a speech: How It Feels to Be a Teacher. I could even talk to a few teachers. Find out how it really does feel.

"If you want to hold your audience," Mrs. Atkins says, "talk about people. Especially talk about how they feel."

The trouble was I forgot about that when I made up that lame speech that turned the kids off. Oh well, there'll be a next time. When it comes to giving speeches in classes, there's always a next time!

Something to Blush About Then
and Laugh About Now

Miss Hambrick said, "Kirk, we could turn this into an assignment." (Why do teachers want to turn everything into an assignment?)

Anyway, this one turned out to be fun. Several kids in our Human Behavior class told about times when they made fools of themselves—their streaks of Charlie Brownness.

Sophie Gannon told about how she got her finger caught in the top of a Coke bottle on her way to class one day. Her finger kept swelling, and she didn't have time to work it out of the bottle because the bell was about to ring. She had to be on time to that class because she'd already been late so often. So she went into class with that Coke bottle dangling from her finger.

What about you? Were you ever a Charlie Brown? Share it with one of your classes. Your teacher might even give you an A.

7

Your Need Got in My Way

We spent two or three days in Human Behavior class talking about needs. Problems crop up when different people's needs bump into each other. We came up with some examples: Someone steals food from a store because he's hungry. That's a *physical* need; it has to do with the body. When someone steals the food, it gets in the way of the storekeeper's need, which is to make a living. That's also a physical need.

A parent's greatest need is to be a good parent. That's an *emotional* need; it has to do with the mind instead of with the body. That means the way we think about something or the way we feel about it. Mr. Rickman says emotional needs are called "psychological" needs. A teenager's need is to prove he's growing up and away from his parents. (Another emotional need.) Smash! The parent's need and the teenager's don't go together.

Maybe they do, though, Mr. R. says. If kids show they can be depended on, the parents figure they are doing an okay job of parenting. So then they relax and give their children more freedom. That sounds pretty good. The trouble is kids are likely to do dumb things to show they aren't taking orders from adults anymore.

Like, for instance, my mom and dad really dig good grades. Makes us look like a family of brains. So that's their need. Now if I get good grades, it'll look as if I'm doing it for them, so I said in class that maybe I could get low grades to prove I'm me.

"Oh, you could, could you?" Mr. Rickman said. "Let's just see how smart that kind of figuring is. Your parents are already out of school. They don't have to worry about their grades. But with a few more failures, you'll be serving time around here after your classmates have left the place behind."

"But how am I supposed to let my mom and dad know I'm not a little kid anymore?" I asked.

"By getting decent grades for one thing," he said. "Little kids can't handle middle-school subjects. Passing classes is a sign of growing up."

Lance asked how we can act grown-up when we always have to let people know where we are.

"There's this little matter of worry," Mr. R. explained. "Your parents know you stand a chance of being in a car accident. That's scary. They know half of highway deaths involve drinking drivers, and they know many teenagers drink. So do many adults who are driving. Your parents have read that only one teen marriage in four makes it. They know of teen girls who get pregnant. Teenagers are among the many people dying of AIDS. Some kids blow their minds on dope and wind up in trouble or in mental hospitals. Your parents are scared, and they have a right to be."

"Yeah, but we can't stay home in our rooms forever just because our folks are scared something's going to happen to us," Daren argued.

"No, but you can come in when you're supposed to. You can get on the phone and check in from time to time. Caring people don't go out of their way to worry others. Responsible people can be counted on; they build trust."

So that's how that conversation wound up. Mr. Rickman would be more fun to argue with if he didn't make so much sense. Oh well! He's a great teacher even if he does make too much sense.

Something to Notice

Our homework assignment was to check out the people around us. In our families, our classes, club meetings, in the halls, on the street, wherever. When we notice people having trouble getting along together, we're supposed to see if we can figure out if it's on account of having different needs from each other.

I found a lot of examples. For instance, my mom and I had an argument about my room. It's important for her to have the whole house neat. "A place for everything and everything in its place" is her motto. That's not mine. I figure a place for everything, and nothing in its place. (That's supposed to be a a joke, but it doesn't get any laughs out of my mom.) I like my room with everything out in the open so I don't have to waste time putting stuff away and getting it out again.

Another example was some guy passing our school bus while its red lights were flashing. Our driver's job is to guard the safety of kids. The fellow who zoomed past probably felt he needed to get somewhere in a hurry. Anyhow, the bus driver turned in the guy's license number.

The orchestra teacher and the speech teacher at our school had an argument. They both wanted to use the stage on the same evening. When they saw me watching them, they quit fighting long enough to give me a crusty glare. I didn't stick around to see how it came out.

It's quite a bit of fun to watch other people hassling.

Mr. R. says next time we don't get our own way about something to ask ourselves what needs are getting pushed around.

When was the last time one of your needs got bumped into? Tell your class about it. (If it's okay with your teacher, that is.)

8

If Only...

On Monday morning Mr. Rickman greeted our class with one of his attention getters: "Let's declare this a special week."

Naturally we were curious, so we settled down right away for once.

"There's National Education Week, Fire Prevention Week, and other specially designated ones. Why shouldn't we create our own in this class?"

We still sat there waiting to hear just what this week was going to be. I wasn't sure we wanted to know.

Mr. R. ought to be a mystery-story writer with the way he knows how to keep you in suspense. Finally he let us in on his big idea: "I'd like to call this 'If-Only Week'."

Now we were listening—even Rusty, who usually snoozes through classes.

Mr. R. said: "This peaceful silence is what a teacher dreams of. It would be great if the school principal or a school-board member came to visit at a moment like this."

We knew he was joking. Mr. R. worries that if things are too quiet in a classroom, there's not much learning going on. I wish more teachers thought that way.

Anyway we laughed, but not for long. Before we had a chance to get out of hand, Mr. R. went on to explain about his if-only-week idea. "I've been hearing a lot of lamenting going on lately."

I didn't know what *lamenting* meant, but I didn't ask. I figured everyone else in the class probably did know. Anyway, Mr. R. went on to explain.

"It seems to me people are doing more looking backward than ahead," he said.

"Can you give us an example?" Matt asked.

23

"Several." Mr. R. took a stack of papers from the top of his desk and gave each of us one. Nothing was on the paper except two words followed by a blank line. The two words were *If only.*

"*If only* is a looking-backward phrase," Mr. R. explained. "We're going to think of others. We'll make a list of such phrases and leave a blank line or two after each one to be filled in later."

It took us a while to clue in to what we were supposed to do, but the teacher gave us some ideas. He said, "Think of things people say when they wish they had done something differently. For example: 'If only I had gone out for football.'"

Rusty scribbled something on a slip of paper and put it on my desk.

"I see Rusty is already working on the assignment," Mr. R. said. "Do you want to read it out loud, Kirk?"

"I probably shouldn't," I said, "but it really is sort of funny."

"Lighten my day," Mr. R. said.

I couldn't keep from snickering, and I couldn't resist reading Rusty's comment out loud: "If only I hadn't come to school today."

Mr. Rickman sighed. "If only he hadn't. Now let's get on with this list, thinking of other ways to start a sentence of regret for what has happened. For example, 'I wish I had...'."

Nedra piped up with "Why didn't I....?

"Now you're with it," Mr. R. told her.

That spurred the rest of us on. We finally had a list:

If only....

I wish I had....

I wish I hadn't....

Why didn't I...?

If only I had....

Whatever made me...?

What was I thinking of...?

How could I have known...?

What possessed me to...?

I should have known....

Something to Think About

Mr. Rickman told us to hang on to our lists and try to add to them during the week. You who are reading this might want to add to our looking-back phrases.

Lance asked if we were supposed to complete the sentences.

Mr. Rickman nodded. "That's the main part of the activity. Listen to the people around for if-only kinds of laments."

Evan said: "I already have one. I wish I had studied for a math test I have today."

"Poor kid," Mr. R. said.

Margarita asked what if we didn't hear anyone saying any of those things.

Mr. Rickman's answer to that was: "Then listen to yourself. Pay attention to any such laments you might express during the week. Like Evan's lament. If there aren't any, remember back to times when you did some suffering because you hadn't looked ahead. If that fails, make up some examples or find them in your reading."

"In other words, do this assignment," Rusty threw in.

"You've got it!" Mr. R. said.

You readers out there don't have to do it, but you might want to. It turned out to be sort of interesting.

9

Right for Each Other?

The trouble with being fourteen is, you don't feel like a child, but you keep being treated like one. People are forever reminding you how ungrown-up you are.

That's why John is one of the favorite people in my life.

"I don't know what you see in John," my parents are always saying.

What I see in John is a kid two years older than me and in high school. John and I have been best friends since grade school. The question I keep asking myself is, What does John see in me?

It started out with our living only a few houses away from each other and riding the school bus together. Thinking back to when we were kids, I realize John was my hero because he was always doing risky things like running away from home sometimes and using raunchy language. I even used some of those words when I was with him. John is that kind of person we envy a little—someone who dares to do things you wouldn't think of doing yourself.

I was at John's house once when he ordered thirteen pizzas delivered to the house next door where a cranky old gal who hated children lived. I never quit feeling guilty about that, even though it wasn't my idea, and I didn't make the phone call. In fact, I didn't even hang around until the pizzas were delivered. I knew Mrs. Witch would figure John was the culprit and probably me along with him.

It took me quite a while to realize what I was to John: his audience. I should write a book called *I Grew Up Laughing* because I thought John was a regular comedian. I might add that all this time my folks weren't laughing.

By the time I finally got into middle school where John already was, we had quit being dumb little kids. By that time we were so used to each other that our friendship lasted, even though John doesn't live in my neighborhood anymore.

Whoever said opposites attract was right on.

Anyway my feelings about John explain why I was really looking forward to a hot date he had lined up for us. It happened like this: John and his new girlfriend Ginny were going to the homecoming dance at the high school and wanted to double-date.

I stuttered around, explaining that I wasn't exactly going around with anyone.

Somehow I couldn't see any of the girls from my class on a date with John. Not that I was ashamed of him, of course.... Well, somehow he didn't quite seem to fit in with the crowd I hang out with.

No problem, John assured me. He already had someone lined up for me, Ginny's friend, Shannon Lancaster. I liked the name right away. Sounded like someone you'd write a poem about. Maybe I'd even like the babe. Still, why did John choose me for this date I kept wondering? Why not one of the guys at high school?

So why not just go ahead and ask him instead of stewing around about it? "Why would a high-school girl want to go out with a kid from middle school?" I asked.

John said, "If you're worrying about whether she's a dog or not, forget it. Shannon's a regular turn-on if you know what I mean."

I was afraid I did.

"So quit frowning. I pointed you out to Shannon one day after school when you were at that swimming meet at our building. Shannon thinks you're kinda cute."

There are several things I'd rather be than "kinda cute," but if that was my ticket into high-school social life, I'd settle for it.

"Besides, you're tall," John added, "so you look older than you are."

"Do I have to wear a tux or something?" I asked.

"Something," John said, "but not a tux. You don't have to put on the dog. Just something sort of, you know, *in*." He looked me up and down as if he meant something besides what I usually wear.

Once I agreed to go on the double date, I started stressing out all over again. I know girls' parents get all uptight about their daughters going out with older men. Now the question was, how were my parents going to react to me dating an older woman?

There was one way to find out.

"I have a date to the high-school homecoming dance Friday night," I announced at the supper table. (I had already told my mom she makes the best stew in the world.)

"Why would you be going to a high-school function?" Dad asked.

"John invited me. We're going to double-date."

"You mean you're going with a high-school girl?" From my mother's voice, you'd have thought I had said I was going with a *Playboy* centerfold. She shook her head. "I don't know—"

"Mom, there's nothing to know. I'm fourteen years old, and I have a date for a school dance."

"But with John—" my mom began.

"John is my friend, and he isn't that squirrelly kid he used to be."

"I know, but he's so much older than you. When I was your age, I wasn't allowed to date until I was sixteen."

"No, and the schools weren't handing out free condoms along with textbooks to their pure, innocent little pupils."

My dad jumped into the conversation at that point. "All right, that's enough. There's no need for sarcasm." He turned to my mother. "Maybe it'll be a good experience for him. Find out how older kids act."

I was hoping *Dad* didn't find out before Friday how older kids act.

Something to Compare

The business about John and me gave me a brilliant idea for a description I was supposed to write for English. In our class we've been studying about short stories. Mrs. Atkins says one thing that makes a story interesting is that not all the characters are alike.

"What makes it a story," she said, "is that the characters are in conflict. You could say they aren't just right for each other."

Our assignment was to describe someone we like or know very well who is different from us. We were supposed to tell some of the qualities of that person that appeal to us and some qualities that turn us off. Writing about John was a cinch, so I decided to include our relationship in this book. Miss Hambrick liked working on this chapter with me.

But You Like That Person Anyway?

Who is that someone in your life you shouldn't get along with but do? Is the person good for you? Can you have him or her for a friend and keep on being you? Writing or talking about it in one of your classes could be worth some credit. At least it worked for me in Mrs. Atkins's class.

Talking or writing about the person (don't use their real name, though) can help you to know that person better, help you to see the person more clearly.

10

Evening on the Rocks

It was supposed to be a great evening.

I had pinned John down about what he meant by wearing something that's "in." He said you can usually wear practically anything to the high-school dances as long as it's not something your mother picked out. However, since this is the homecoming dance, it's the custom to dress up more (the girls' idea) and to go out to dinner before the dance.

He said Ginny and Shannon love to look glamorous, so he and I should wear cords or dress pants. We finally decided to rent red cummerbunds and white shirts with all those little pleats down the front. That meant jackets, of course. I happen to have a light brownish one that I never wear. (It was my mother's choice, but I didn't tell John that.)

I rode my bike to John's house feeling ridiculous. I stuck to the alleys, though, so I don't think anyone saw me.

John and I laughed at each other in our dress-up gear. I was already wishing I hadn't let myself get talked into this.

John's mother told us how handsome we looked, and John's dad gave us each a beer. I must have got a funny look on my face. Mr. Roper pointed to the word *Lite* on the beer can.

"We believe in teaching our son to do his drinking at home," he explained. I thought that was like saying you give your five-year-old candy at home so he won't eat it anywhere else.

I knew I ought to have said we shouldn't drink before driving, but the words just wouldn't come out. I didn't feel anything after the beer, though, so decided John probably didn't either.

As it turned out, that evening was full of bummers for me. This scene at the Roper house was one of them. I described it in Human Behavior class when we were talking about choices. We tried to decide if there was some way I could have handled the situation better. Most of the class thought I couldn't have, because it was an adult who offered the beer in his own home. Adults would probably say I should have backed out and gone home at that point. Or I should have refused the beer. My classmates didn't think so though.

We picked the girls up at Ginny's house. I hadn't felt a buzz when I drank the beer, but I did the minute I saw Shannon. Here was the doll who had thought I was "kinda cute," and she looked at me as if she still thought so.

Later, when I tried to describe Shannon to Miss Hambrick for this chapter, I had a lot of trouble finding the words. "She has all this hair," I said. "Not brown or red exactly."

"Auburn," Miss Hambrick suggested.

"And her eyes are green," I went on, "and they sort of poke up at the corners. Not both corners, that is, but at the ends."

Miss Hambrick smiled and patted my shoulder. "How about *tilted a bit at the outer corners?*"

"Right," I said. "And her skin isn't dark, but it isn't very light either."

"Ivory," Miss Hambrick decided.

So that's the way Shannon looks. But what was different about her was that she made me feel as if I was the person she really wanted to be with at that minute.

We went to this classy place to eat. The fluffs seemed impressed, but I was dreading how much of a hole it would put in my wallet. To make matters worse, John told the waitress to bring us a wine list.

She said: "Ha! Ask me again when you're twenty-one."

John punched his charm button. He smiled and leaned close to the gal, who was fairly old — about the age of our mothers — and whispered, "I suppose you wouldn't settle for a nonalcoholic —"

"You suppose right," she interrupted. "Those so-called nonalcoholic drinks contain alcohol."

"But not enough —" John began.

This time it was Ginny who cut him off. "We'll settle for Cokes."

"Make mine coffee," John said.

As soon as the waitress disappeared, John began to complain. "How does she know we're minors? Didn't even card us." He gave me a slap on the shoulder and laughed. "It was prob'ly you she was looking at, Kirky-boy."

I wanted to slide under the table. So this was the kid whose parents wanted him to do his drinking at home.

Shannon said, "Shut up and see if you can read the menu."

John gave a snort. "Well, I never had French, but...."

"Just order a cheeseburger," I suggested. I was wishing there *was* something like a cheeseburger or taco on the list.

We finally settled for the least expensive item on the menu, chicken catch-something-or-other. ("Cacciatore," Miss Hambrick said when we worked on the chapter.)

As soon as the waitress left, John pulled a flask out of his pocket. "Now for a little Irish coffee," he said. The next thing we knew he was doctoring his coffee with a splash of whiskey or whatever was in the flask. He laughed. "Irish coffee without the whipped cream," he whispered.

I looked around nervously, but no one was paying attention to us. The girls and I sat there like a bunch of dumb kindergartners while John proceeded to put whiskey in our Cokes.

Ginny put her hand over her glass. "You can skip me; I'll be driving."

"Then I'll take your share," John said, adding another swish to his cup.

During the meal John started talking loud and doing a lot of bragging. A couple of times he added a slosh or two of liquor to his "Irish coffee."

The waitress finally brought our check on a little brown tray. "I'll pick it up in a minute," she said.

We looked at each other some more. Then finally John and I got out our wallets and fumbled around counting out the right amount plus a five-dollar tip.

There go a couple of pizzas, I was thinking with a last look at the tip.

John added a final shake of whiskey to his coffee and drained his cup.

"You'd better lay off that stuff," I told him.

"Hey, c'mon, man. This night's special."

"You can't drink and drive," I said, sounding like a panicky little kid.

"Let's go," Shannon said, standing up.

Ginny said: "Give me the keys. I'll drive."

From that point, the evening was a disaster with a capital *D*.

John got to feeling sorry for himself in the car and finally started to bawl. None of us knew how to handle that. I'd been around kids when they were drinking, but I'd never seen one act like this, and I'd never been with John when he was drinking.

"Good grief, he's wasted," Shannon said disgustedly.

"He's not usually like this," Ginny said in a shaky voice.

"How long have you been going with this guy, Ginny?" Shannon asked.

"A few weeks," Ginny answered in the same shaky voice. "He's Kirk's friend."

Shannon glared at me. "Well, after this, we'd better check out who our friends are before we include them in our plans."

"Quit sounding like my mother," I told her. "I happen to like the guy."

I didn't really. Not right then anyway. I wanted to kill him.

In the school parking lot we finally got John quieted down and looking fairly normal.

"Shall we go in?" I asked.

Shannon said: "Might as well, I suppose. As long as we're here." I figured she wanted to show off her dress and all that hair. I couldn't really blame her.

Ginny put her nose in the air and walked ahead of us.

"Sorry, guys," John kept saying. "Musta had a little too much. Sorry."

"Shut up!" I told him. "And keep your mouth shut when we go in. You smell like a wino."

Shannon and Ginny refused to dance with John, but he latched onto another girl and proceeded to make an idiot of himself with a bunch of fancy steps. The girl's date came over and told John to get lost. Then John got belligerent and started to tell the guy off.

I could see a man—the school principal or someone—heading in our direction, so I grabbed John by the sleeve and yanked him toward the door. Ginny and Shannon followed, and we managed to get John to the car.

At this point, all we wanted was to get home, but the question was, Who would drop who off where? It was John's car, but we weren't about to let him drive. I didn't have a driver's license, so that left the girls. We finally decided Ginny would drive. She'd drop John and me off at his house since my bike was there. Then the girls would go on to Ginny's house, where Shannon was spending the night.

"But what about my car?" John asked, sounding pretty foggy.

"I'll get it to you tomorrow," Ginny told him. "Now pour yourself into the backseat with Kirk."

So that's how my first big-time date ended. I steered John from the car to his porch, then took off on my bike as soon as the door closed behind him.

Good-bye Shannon, I thought. Do you still think I'm kinda cute?

If Only....

I made a list of if only's for Mr. Rickman.

Mr. R. had our class do some role-playing about each part of the evening. First we played it the way it happened, then how some of the mess might have been avoided. Here's my list:

If only I hadn't let John talk me into going on a date with older kids.

Why didn't I tell John and his parents I'm not old enough to drink? (I know I'd have never done this one. It would make me sound like a little kid.)

I wish I'd grabbed the flask away from John at the table. (Can you see a kid doing that?)

I should have insisted that Ginny drive John home from the restaurant instead of our going on to the dance.

What on earth possessed us to go into the dance when John was obviously drunk?

And finally one I didn't put on the list I handed to Mr. Rickman, but here it is for the book: If only I could make myself call Shannon and tell her John's really a cool dude. I doubt if she'd believe me.

And here's one for the present instead of the past: If only I had the nerve to tell Shannon I'd like to see her again.

11

My Best Friend: One in Three Million

When we say somebody's one in a million, that usually means the person is really great. But John's being one in three million doesn't mean he's three times greater than great; it means he's probably one of the three million teenagers in our country who could be classified as alcoholic. That means being addicted to alcohol.

It's one thing to know facts about drinking, like two hundred thousand kids between ages fifteen and nineteen are involved in alcohol-related accidents every year, and five thousand of these die. It's something else to watch a friend's drinking ruin a fabulous evening.

I didn't hear anything from John for a week after the dance. That was okay with me. Maybe we were outgrowing each other. In a way it was a relief, but there was also a big, empty hole in my life.

Then just when I was getting used to the idea of no more John, he called me up: "Hi, there, old buddy. I've been meaning to call and thank you for double-dating with me and Ginny."

"Sure," I said, wondering how he could be so casual about it.

"Ginny's been real cool toward me since that evening. I hope I didn't make a fool of myself."

"Don't you *remember*?" I asked.

"Well, no. Not after the restaurant. I know this sounds dumb, but after a few drinks I sort of blot out. Can't remember from nothin'."

"But aren't you afraid of what will happen?"

"Oh come off it, Kirk. You sound like a stuffy minister. Practically all the kids drink, you know."

I said: "Well sure, but at least they know what's going on. Anyway, I do." I wasn't about to admit I'm not into drinking. Not yet, anyway. Maybe never,

34

after seeing what alcohol's doing to some of my friends and their families.

"Well, maybe you don't drink as much as I do," John said.

"Why don't you stop before you drink too much?" I asked.

John gave a nervous laugh. "The funny thing is I don't *know* when to stop. Just keep chuggin' it down."

"Don't your folks get onto you when you come in smashed?"

"Hell, no. One night when I came home that way, Dad got sort of panicky and wanted to know if I was on drugs. When I told him I'd just had a few beers, he acted real relieved."

I could imagine my parents being relieved over a drunk son! They'd freak out if they even knew I had that beer at John's house and the spiked Coke at the restaurant.

I kept thinking about what John had told me. Sure, I know guys get poured into bed now and then, but there was something different about John's drinking. I couldn't figure out what it was though. After all, a drunk is a drunk.

Then suddenly I remembered something that had happened a couple of years ago when John was still at our school. I passed the principal's office one morning and heard someone bawling inside. Some girl, I thought. Girls cry over everything. Somehow it didn't sound like a girl though. I hung around by the counter pretending I was waiting to use the phone. Since there's always a waiting line a block long, I knew I'd be there for a while.

All of a sudden John's dad came rushing into the office and said to the secretary: "I understand my son is in some sort of difficulty. Someone called me."

"Oh yes, Mr. Roper. The principal is expecting you." Ms. Murphy knocked on Mrs. Courtney's door. When the door was opened, I saw John sitting there looking like a slob and bawling like a calf. I can still remember the rest of the scene. It went something like this:

Mr. Roper yelled, "What's this all about?" He pushed the door, but it didn't go all the way shut, so those of us waiting for the phone got in on the floor show.

I heard Mrs. Courtney telling Mr. Roper that his son had come to school drunk that morning.

"Nonsense!" Mr. Roper bellowed.

"It doesn't happen to be nonsense," Mrs. Courtney's voice said. "John fell out of his seat in class and vomited on the floor."

"Well, I'll knock his block off if it's true," Mr. Roper said.

About that time someone clicked the door to Mrs. Courtney's office shut, so the excitement was over for us eavesdroppers.

The scene kept nagging at me all day, so at supper I brought it up.

"What would you guys do if I went to school drunk?"

"Kirk!" my mother shrieked.

"I didn't plan to; I just wondered how you'd react."

"Why do you ask?" my dad wanted to know.

"Gee, can't anybody ever just answer a question?" I asked in my you're-picking-on-me voice.

"Well, I'll answer that one," Dad said. "Things would be pretty uncomfortable around here for a while."

"Would you threaten to knock my block off?"

"Have I ever?"

"No."

"I still wonder why you brought it up," my mom said.

"A kid was drunk at school today, and they called his dad to come." I went ahead and told them what I'd heard, but I didn't say the kid was John.

"A boy who goes to school drunk needs help," my mother said.

After that conversation, I put the whole thing out of my mind for the time being. After all, John in trouble wasn't exactly news.

Now two years later it came rushing back into my mind, especially my mom saying "A boy who goes to school drunk needs help."

John's voice on the phone brought me back to now. "Hey, are you still there?"

"I'm here," I said. Somehow I had to get across to John a message about drinking too much. The only thing that came to my mind to say was, "By the way, Rory Gore got sent off to a rehab center for kids who are alcoholics."

"Who, for cripes sake, is Rory Gore?"

"A boy in one of my classes," I said. "A kid my age."

John laughed. "Come off it, Kirk. Kids aren't alcoholics."

"A lot of them are," I said. "Like more than three million in our country. We learned that in my science class."

John laughed again. "Well, that's not us."

"Maybe it could be," I said. "About one drinker in ten turns out not to be able to stop drinking. That's a lot of kids right here in our own schools."

John quit laughing and sounded definitely impatient. "Well, come out of your pulpit, Reverend, and let's talk about something that has to do with us."

Lecturing people about what they ought to do isn't my thing, but I felt as if I was trying to keep someone from drowning. How could I get through to this jerk? I remembered something Mrs. Atkins told us in English class one day. She said when we give our speeches in class to try to end them with something that will stay in the listeners' minds after we quit talking. Like planting a seed.

So I dug around for a seed and came up with a brilliant one, of course. "Say, John, if you knew you were that one person in ten who will become an alcoholic, would you keep on drinking?"

Of course, he didn't answer. Just changed the subject. So much for brilliance. Will John be the one in ten? Only John can answer that, I guess.

Something to Share

I'm always surprised at how the subject of alcohol gets everyone started talking. It might be at home or in a class or in a group-counseling session. Wherever. It seems everyone either knows an alcoholic or wants to tell about something connected with alcohol.

Mr. Slovoski, my science teacher, says that isn't strange considering there are eleven million alcoholics in our country, and for each one of those, an average of four other people are seriously affected. That doesn't count all the accidents and sickness and lost time at work and other results of moderate drinking.

Some of the topics we talked about in social studies class were:

1. an alcoholic in the family;

2. alcohol and driving (including planes, boats, trains, and other vehicles);

3. alcohol's effects on behavior;

4. alcohol's effects on the body, including the brain;

5. alcohol's role in suicide;

6. Alcoholics Anonymous; Al-Anon, Alateen, and other rehab programs for problem drinkers and their families;

7. child and teen use and abuse of alcohol;

8. alcohol's role in crime;

9. alcohol on the job;

10. alcohol in the schools;

11. the alcoholic blackout; and

12. FAS (Fetal Alcohol Syndrome); the effects of alcohol on the unborn child.

The topic about the alcoholic blackout was the one I paid the most attention to because it made me understand John's problem better. I brought up the subject in Human Behavior class one day.

Mr. Rickman explained that the blackout isn't the same as when a person passes out from drinking too much. In a blackout, the drinker goes ahead and says and does things, but afterward can't remember a bit of what happened. Like one man drove several people home from a meeting one night, and the next day he wondered how they got home. Mr. R. says people often have accidents during blackouts. He says the blackout is a definite danger signal, a true warning that the person is alcoholic.

I decided to show off by bringing a really heavy quotation to Human Behavior class the next day. The longest one I could find was something a psychiatrist named Dr. Will Meninger said. I practiced reading it several times before I laid it on the class. Here's what the doctor says:

> Alcoholism is a character disorder marked by repeated excessive drinking to such a degree that the individual's own efficiency or happiness is severely impaired and the relationships in his family, in his business and with his friends are jeopardized.

That might impress a teacher into boosting my grade, but the class just sat there looking bored. The kids did come back to life, though, when Mr. Rickman said, "An alcoholic can't stop drinking once he's had one drink."

12

Why Take It Out on Me?

What a bummer of a day Tuesday was. Bad news starting with breakfast.

"Can't you ever be on time?" my dad asked as his greeting to me.

"Not only that, but the way you look," my mother put in. "We aren't exactly bankrupt, you know."

"This is the way we dress nowadays," I told her.

"Since when do you have to be like everyone else?" Dad asked.

"Well, you *are* supposed to dress like other people your age. You dress like all those other middle-aged nuts."

The words hung there in the air between my parents and me. This was what Mrs. Atkins means when she talks about handing someone a thistle. What I had said made good sense. That didn't count, though, because of the way I said it.

Dad looked furious, which wasn't as bad as Mom looking hurt. She said, "Since you want to be like your classmates, maybe you'd like to see your name on the honor roll like Jeff Peters."

Jeff Peters! I wanted to say something awful about him, like how he's a geek or that no one likes him. The trouble is, he isn't a geek and people do like him. Not just other grown-ups, but kids too.

"Maybe Jeff's smarter than me," I suggested.

"There's nothing wrong with your ability—" Dad began.

I interrupted him. "So here we go with that old song and dance about how teachers say I don't work up to what I could do."

"You don't have to yell," Mother said. "The neighbors already know you have a temper."

"Oh, they do, do they? Well, the neighbors can go to—"

"Kirk!" My parents broke in before I had a chance to say where the neighbors could go. They both looked as if they were about to have a stroke.

"I'm getting out of here!" I yelled. I went out and slammed the door. The school counselor, Mr. Dean, would say I was running away from the problem, and sure enough I was.

Letting off all that steam should have made me feel great, but it didn't. I felt really bummed during first-period class — social studies, not my favorite subject. To make it worse, Miss Roylston was in a crabby mood. The class was even more boring than usual.

I forgot all about promising myself to look interested in class. I started turning the pages of a magazine.

"Kirk!" The way Miss Roylston cracked out my name you'd have thought I had set the room on fire. "Go to the office," she ordered.

"To the *office*! What for?"

"You appear to have no wish to be in class."

"I have no wish to be in the office either," I said.

Ted snickered, and that really set the teacher off. "Ted, you may go with him."

"What do I say when I get to the office?" I asked. "That I was looking at a magazine?"

Miss Roylston said, "Just tell them I've had it up to the eyebrows with students who do not take part in class."

I tried to think of something clever to say, but Ted was already on his way out the door. "C'mon," he said. "Anything would beat this."

Ms. Murphy, the secretary in the office, looked at us as if we were stray dogs. "What do you boys want?"

"To see the principal," we told her.

"She's at a meeting," Ms. Murphy said.

"Then we'll settle for the vice principal," I said, trying to sound important.

Ms. Murphy said: "Oh, you will, will you? That depends on whether he wants to see you or not."

"Well, go find out," Ted told her.

Ms. Murphy boiled over at that point. "Say, young man, my job isn't taking orders from you. Maybe you'd *better* see the vice principal. He's the one who's in charge of discipline anyway."

"Boy, isn't everyone jolly today?" I commented, while Ms. Murphy went to tell Mr. Cramer about us.

Mr. Cramer was reading a letter and frowning when we went into his office. He didn't look exactly overjoyed to see us. "What seems to be the trouble?" he asked.

"Miss Roylston sent us to the office."

"What for?"

"Nothing," I said. "We weren't doing a thing."

Mr. Cramer said, "Maybe that's why you're here."

"That's what she said," I admitted. "She's tired of kids who don't take part in class."

"So am I," Mr. Cramer said. "Here I am faced with an important matter." He thumped his fingers against the letter on his desk. "Now I'm forced to stop and deal with a couple of students who refuse to work. I'm going to suspend you boys for a day or so until you decide whether or not you want to be in school."

"Suspend us!" I shouted. "For nothing?"

"That's about it." Mr. Cramer was already dialing the phone to let our parents know that we were being suspended for the rest of the day. He said we would get back into school when they came with us for a conference.

That's all I needed. A day at home with my mother, who was already torked at me.

"Now see what you got me into," Ted said in a snarly tone as we left the office.

So now even Ted was mad at me. All this hassle over nothing.

I stayed out of my mother's way as much as possible, and she didn't have much to say. Just went around looking hurt, as if I'd turned out to be a real flop. I was glad my dad had left after breakfast on a business trip, so I didn't have to face him that night. He wasn't home to go to school with Mom and me the next morning for the meeting with Mr. Cramer.

As it turned out, Miss Roylston was there too. So was Mr. Dean, because a counselor usually sits in on conferences that have to do with discipline.

First, Miss Roylston explained what happened. She said she was sorry for being so upset with Ted and me. "I lashed out too strongly," she admitted.

I remembered that she had been having some problems with several kids lately. Maybe when I acted bored, she got worried about losing control of the class. So then she exploded, and I happened to be the target.

Mr. Dean said: "It's that time of the school year when tempers are getting short. Sometimes things seem to be worse than they are. Instead of being the boss of our emotions, we let them rule us. Then we say and do things we would like to erase later on."

Mom said: "Come to think of it, I was short with Kirk before he left for school yesterday. Sent him off in a bad frame of mind."

It appeared to be time for confessions, so I put in my bit. "If I hadn't already been mad at my parents, I probably wouldn't have taken it out on Miss Roylston by acting as if I didn't care about the class."

"What were you upset with your parents about, Kirk?" Mr. Dean asked. "Is it something you want to discuss?"

"Sure. Why not? I got the feeling they were comparing me to another kid. Wanting me to be smarter than I am."

"We were doing that," my mother admitted. "And we shouldn't."

"What kind of comparison were you making?" Mr. Cramer asked.

Mom said: "About grades, for one thing. We know school work isn't easy for Kirk, but sometimes we worry that he isn't trying hard enough to do his best. But the funny thing about it is, I don't think it was Kirk I was upset with. The other day one of my friends was bragging about her son's being on the honor roll. I think *she's* the one I was annoyed with. Kirk, the truth is your dad and I wouldn't trade you for anyone."

I was remembering that Mom and Dad had been quarreling the evening before they chewed on me. They were hollering about Dad's being out of town so much. Maybe they lit into me because they were griped at each other.

I said: "Mr. Dean, I just remembered something you said in one of our group sessions. We were talking about anger. You said it jumps around like lightning, hitting the wrong people sometimes."

"That's about it," Mr. Cramer agreed. "I'll admit I was anything but understanding when Ted and Kirk came to my office. I had a heavy decision to make. All I could think of was getting rid of the boys. Suspending them was not a good way to handle the problem."

"Maybe it was," Mr. Dean said. "It got us together to tell how we feel about a few things. It's a chance to express ourselves without getting hurt or hurting someone else."

"How do you feel about things now, Kirk?" Mr. Cramer asked.

"Better," I said. "I was pretty burned up yesterday. The things I said didn't come out very well."

So that's how the meeting ended, with people feeling all right about one another again. I thought about how any one of us—my parents, me, Miss Roylston, Mr. Cramer—could have prevented the whole bad scene by saying the right thing at some point along the way.

Well, we didn't, and I guess that's because we're human beings who get hurt pretty easy. Maybe the next time we'll be in control of our feelings instead of the other way around.

Something to Salvage from a Bad Scene

I'm so used to having teachers turn our everyday problems into assignments that I decided to do that with this one. Write a chapter for the book, Kirk, I told myself. Okay, I answered. And this was it.

13

See What You Made Me Do!

Once a week a group of us students gets together with our counselor, Mr. Dean, for a spilling-over session. It's a great chance to say some things we're feeling without getting into trouble.

For this chapter and any others about our counseling group I had to get permission from Mr. Dean and the group members to tape what we said, since counseling sessions are supposed to be private. "Confidential," Mr. Dean calls it. The group said sure go ahead if it can be of any use to anyone who might read the book. Mr. Dean said I must not use our real names, though, so I made up the names except for Mr. Dean's and mine.

This week we started off with our usual gripes about parents, teachers, rules, and stuff.

Mr. Dean wasn't in a very good mood. Just when we were getting wound up, he interrupted us. "I see you're going to waste another hour playing the game of See What You Made Me Do," he said.

"I thought we were supposed to get things off our chests," Morris said. "Tell how we feel. Talk about what's stressing us out."

"Sure, go right ahead," Mr. Dean said.

"Well, I did have some things I wanted to talk about," Allison said in a whiny voice.

"So what's stopping you?" Sally asked.

"I don't know whether I should. After what Mr. Dean said about playing See What You Made Me Do."

Mr. Dean said: "Suppose you go ahead, Allison. Maybe then I can show you what I mean."

Nobody has to twist Allison's arm to get her to talk. All she has to do is open her mouth. Allison's life belongs on TV with the soap operas.

"I'm flunking all my classes," she began.

"Seems a little silly, since you are in courses you can handle," Mr. Dean told her.

"Well, I can't concentrate on my studies. If you lived around our house, you'd see why. My dad drunk half the time. My mother always complaining about being sick. My brother in trouble. I'd just as well give up."

"What are your plans for when you finish school? In case you ever do, that is," Mr. Dean wanted to know.

"How can I make plans in a setup like that? My mother claims she's sick on account of me, and—"

"How come on account of you?" Rob interrupted.

"She says it's because I come in late at night and keep the family worried all the time and don't help around the house. If you ask me, it's my dad's drinking that makes her sick. Makes my brother and me do what we're not supposed to too. My dad claims he drinks because of my mother always complaining and my brother being in trouble and me keeping him worried."

"Sounds as if the whole family is playing See What You Made Me Do," Mr. Dean said.

"Well, *I'm* not playing any old game!" Allison said. "What else can I do in a mixed-up family like that one?"

Mr. Dean said: "Suppose we change the name of the game? Call it See What *I* Made Me Do."

"I don't get it," Allison said. She looked annoyed. She doesn't like to have anything get in the way of her raving on about what a rough life she has.

"Suppose you tell us again what you just said about your family problems," Mr. Dean suggested. "Only this time tell it as if it's all your own fault. As if you brought all your problems on yourself."

"But I didn't," Allison insisted.

"Whether you did or not, tell it that way."

Allison sat there sulking for a while. I guess she finally decided she'd do things Mr. Dean's way. That would be better than not to get to babble on about her troubles at all.

"Well, I'm flunking all my classes," she began. "It's my fault, because I don't study. But how *could* anyone study—"

"Oh, oh," Mr. Dean interrupted.

"Oh yes, I forgot," Allison said. "This is hard to do. Especially when—"

"Especially when everything's someone else's fault?" Jean asked. "Is that what you were going to say?"

Allison said: "Okay, okay! So the bad grades are my fault. But about my dad being drunk—"

"Play the game," Mr. Dean reminded her.

"Well, all right then. It's my fault I don't do what I'm supposed to. What my dad does shouldn't keep me from doing what's right."

"Hey, now you're with it," Bill told her.

That really got her going. "Maybe it is partly my fault my dad drinks. He probably figures he failed with me. Maybe that's why my mom is sick so much too. I could help around the house more. I could build my dad up instead of cutting him down. And I could start coming in on time and getting better grades—"

Allison stopped suddenly as if she had just started listening to herself. Finally she said, "But even if I did all that, my dad wouldn't quit drinking and my mom wouldn't quit being sick and my brother would still be in trouble."

"That's right," Mr. Dean said. "All I wanted you people to think about is that you do bring on some of your own problems. Or make them worse."

Sally said, "We have some problems we can't do anything about."

Mr. Dean nodded. "That's right. There are two kinds of problems: those we can't control and those we do have some control over."

"So what do we do about the ones we don't have control over?" I asked.

Mr. Dean explained. "Suppose you are trapped in a bad condition like Allison's family problems. What happens? First of all, you feel helpless. Second, you feel angry. When you are angry, you want to get even with whoever is making your life disagreeable. In getting even, your behavior becomes bad, and people won't put up with it. That means a new set of problems for you. Let's talk about that, Allison, and see how it works in your case."

"Well," Allison began, "I'm trapped with parents who don't act the way parents are supposed to."

"But...." Mr. Dean said.

"But my life with them might not be quite so hopeless if I tried to be a better daughter."

Mr. Dean patted Allison's shoulder. "Good. Now take it from there."

Allison smiled, so she must have begun to like the game. She went on: "Since I'm mad at my parents for being the way they are, I get bad grades and break rules to get even with them. Then I get in trouble with teachers."

Mr. Dean nodded again. "So...."

"So then I have more problems at home and at school," Allison added.

"Besides," I reminded her, "if you keep flunking stuff, you won't graduate when you're s'posed to."

Jean added, "And then you won't be able to get a job. Then you'll be stuck at home even when you're old enough to move out."

"Jeez!" Allison said. "Nobody understands."

Mr. Dean said, "Just see what we're making you do."

Allison laughed. "Oh, all right. So you guys think I ought to solve *some* of my problems."

"Not if it's more fun to feel sorry for yourself," Mr. Dean told her.

"Okay, okay. So I'll start studying and quit breaking rules."

Sally put her arm around Allison, and Rob patted her arm. We were all hoping Allison meant what she said. Maybe we were thinking about what we could do about some of our own problems. In any case, it looks as if we aren't going to get away with any more poor-little-me sessions with Mr. Dean. Sigh!

Something to Do

The kids in our Human Behavior class liked the tape from the group session. They decided it was a game we could play. (Any game usually beats the regular kind of assignments we're used to.) We broke up into groups and did just what Mr. Dean's group did. First we told our problem as if it was other people's fault. Then we did it over, switching to See What I Made Me Do."

We decided blaming yourself is really hard to do, especially when feeling sorry for yourself can be fun.

Something to Notice

One of our assignments was to bring to class examples of people blaming others for their mistakes. Mr. R. said a good source would be to listen to politicians on TV, like the president blaming Congress for things and Congress blaming the president.

We also were to mention times when we blamed someone else for our own problems. One of the hardest things to say is "I made a mistake."

14

Crying's Okay

My parents made me go to school that day even though I felt as if I couldn't stand to be around anyone. Where can you get away from people in a school? Finally I wandered into the room where I have English. No one was there except Mrs. Atkins, and she was busy grading papers.

I sat down across the desk from her. She just looked up at me and smiled as if there was nothing strange about a kid coming to the English room when he didn't have to.

"He's dead," I said in a strangled kind of voice.

"John?"

I nodded. "He was my best bud, even if he was two years older than me."

She said, "I know." She walked over and closed the door, then came back to her desk.

"I miss him," I said.

She nodded. "I know, and that hurts. When something hurts, it's all right to cry." She put a box of tissues in front of me and went on grading papers while I began to bawl. I was relieved that she didn't look at me.

"Nothing like this ever happened to me before," I said. "I don't know how to handle it."

"You don't have much choice," she told me. "John is gone, and he won't be back."

"But what do I do?"

"Just keep on hurting until you begin to heal a little."

"I don't think I'll ever feel like myself again."

"Of course you *know* you will, but right now you can't *believe* you will."

I shook my head.

She said, "It's because we know with our minds, but we believe with our feelings."

I sat and thought about that for a while.

"You might make things easier for John's family by visiting them."

I hadn't thought about John's family until now. If this was rough on me, what must it be for them?

"John's parents don't like me," I explained. "They think I was bad news for him."

"And probably your folks weren't wild about your running around with him."

"That's right." I was surprised at how much Mrs. Atkins seemed to know. Just a plain English teacher.

"That's how it is with parents," she said. "Young people together do things they wouldn't have the nerve to do by themselves. So parents get the idea that their sons and daughters are being led astray by their friends."

"Hey, that's about it."

"Go see John's family, Kirk. They'll change their minds about you now. You'll see. And if they don't, you will at least have given it a try."

"I feel guilty about some of the things John and I did," I said. "Maybe God makes us feel guilty to punish us."

Mrs. Atkins shook her head. "I don't think God plans for us to carry big loads of guilt along through life. We do have a conscience, though, so we can learn from our mistakes."

That seemed to make good sense, but I didn't know how to quit feeling guilty. Mrs. Atkins might have known what I was thinking. She said, "Guilt can be a crutch, you know."

"A crutch?"

"Yes, indeed. Guilt is a sort of self-punishment, so if you feel guilty enough, you don't have to do something about yourself."

"Something about yourself?"

"Like improving your behavior, for instance."

The first bell rang, so I stood up to go.

"By the way," Mrs. Atkins said, "I'm glad you weren't with John in that car when it wrecked."

"That's something else I feel guilty about," I admitted. "About John getting killed and not me."

Mrs. Atkins said, "That's one thing you should not feel guilty about—being alive when someone else dies."

"Oh," I said. "Well, thanks for helping me. My folks didn't understand how I felt."

"How do you know?"

"They forced me to come to school."

"Perhaps that's because they did understand. They probably figured you'd be better off at school with classmates to share your grief."

"Oh, I didn't think about that. I wonder—"

The thought of going to see John's family was the hardest thing I can remember having to do. I wanted to talk to my parents about it, but I was afraid they wouldn't understand. Still, Mrs. Atkins had said they might be more understanding than I realized.

At dinnertime Mom said: "We know you feel bad about John. Is there anything you'd like to talk about?"

That gave me the opening I needed. "I ought to go see John's family, but they probably don't want to see me."

"Why not?" Dad asked.

"On account of how John and I got into trouble sometimes."

"Sorrow sometimes brings people closer together," my mother said. "If I were John's mother, I'd appreciate your coming."

So I forced my legs to take me to John's house. A lady I didn't know opened the door and took me to the living room. John's mother and father and sister sat there like broken dolls, staring into space. I didn't know what to do, but I tried to imagine they were my parents instead of John's.

Then it seemed natural to go over and put my arm across Mrs. Roper's shoulder. When I did that, she began to cry. She put her arm around my waist and her head against my shoulder. "Forgive me for breaking down," she said. "I thought I was all cried out."

I remembered what Mrs. Atkins had said. "It's all right to cry," I told her.

All of a sudden I was crying too. John's sister, Adele, who is eleven, came over then and put her arms around her mother and me. I began to feel sorry for John's dad, sitting all by himself. After a little while I went over to him and put my hand on his arm.

"I'm glad to hear you say it's all right to cry," he said. "I keep wanting to do that."

Some other people came into the room about that time, so I said I guessed I'd better go. Mrs. Roper walked to the door with me. "Kirk, it was so comforting to see you."

"I was afraid you didn't like me."

"We love you because John loved you. And Kirk, don't fret about the past. You and John weren't perfect; you just made some bad choices."

"I'll come again," I promised.

"Oh, Kirk, will you? It would mean so much to us."

I walked home feeling better than I had since that end-of-the-world minute when I heard my best friend was dead. Tomorrow I would tell Mrs.

Atkins about the visit to John's family.

Mrs. Atkins. My parents. John's parents. It's amazing how understanding adults can be at times!

Miss Hambrick and I both cried when we worked on this chapter. She said our biggest hurt is when someone we love dies. That's happening more and more often to kids our age nowadays on account of car accidents, gang warfare, overdosing on drugs and alcohol, AIDS, murder, and all sorts of things. Some children even get killed by their own parents.

At our school, when a pupil or teacher dies, the school counselors and psychologists meet with us kids in groups to help us handle our grief. At a time like that you find out that adults really do care about you.

If a schoolmate or someone else close to you dies, talk about it. Write about it. Don't keep it all sealed up inside of you.

Mr. Dean says grief is an illness. It takes quite a while to get well.

15

Who Has Problems?

The group counseling session over Allison's woes got Mr. Dean started off on a problem-solving kick. First we talked about who has problems. We decided that having problems is the one thing everyone can count on, starting with when we're born. Our concern at that time is to attract someone's attention when we're hungry or wet or sick or uncomfortable.

The baby solves its problem by bawling. As the kid gets older, crying doesn't work so well anymore. So then the little schemer gets smart and tries some other ways of getting attention. Like maybe finding out that smiling and cooing and uttering a few words get some good results.

Mr. Dean says we go through life trying to get people's attention so we won't start feeling like zeros. Bad behavior is a way of saying "Please look at me."

"It also says 'I hurt'," Allison added, and we agreed.

Mr. Dean said if we could put our feelings into words—decent words—we wouldn't have to act out so much and wind up in trouble. He asked Allison if she or her brother had ever tried telling her dad how they felt about his drinking.

"It wouldn't do any good," Allison said.

We just looked at her and didn't say anything.

"At least I don't think it would," she said finally.

That got me to thinking maybe I could tell my mom I don't like it when she cuts my friends down. I could tell her I don't do that about her friends, and some of them really turn me off. I wonder how she'd take it if I said that. Depends on how I say it, I guess.

Mr. Dean says there are really only three ways of dealing with problems: get them solved, which isn't always possible; get away from them, which usually isn't possible; learn to live with them.

We used Allison's problems as examples (with her permission, of course). Chances are, Allison can't solve the problem of her dad's alcoholism, but she could give it a try. Talk to him about the disease. Give him some stuff to read. Suggest he go to some recovery plan, such as Alcoholics Anonymous.

Allison probably can't do much about her mother's ailments either. The sickness may be her mother's way of saying "Look at me for a change." Allison might have some influence over her brother's behavior. For instance, she might talk to him patiently and show him a lot of love. But that might not work either. We decided all of this is worth a try though.

However, if the family doesn't get straightened out, what about walking away from the scene? Wouldn't work, we figure. Allison isn't ready to leave home because she isn't out of school and probably couldn't make a living at this point. Besides, her parents would have the police haul her home.

Should she live with the problem gracefully?

"No way!" Allison said.

"Then you will have to go on living with it ungracefully," Mr. Dean told her. "You've just run out of choices."

We all looked at Allison to see how she'd take that. It's funny how you can get concerned about someone even when you don't especially like the person. I think we were all relieved when Allison said, "I suppose there are some things I could do."

"Like...?" Mr. Dean asked.

Before we knew it, we had a regular workshop going. First, we listed some of Allison's problems: not liking to be at home on account of all the trouble going on there, not being able to keep her mind on homework, not having friends, feeling angry most of the time, not getting along with teachers.

Next we listed some of the pluses—the good things—in Allison's life: good-looking; smart; being healthy in spite of not feeling well a lot of the time; having a home and family, even if they're not just the way she would like for them to be; having an outgoing personality (meaning she's not shy and all scrunched up inside of herself); being able to look at her problems and wanting to do something about them; our being willing to help her.

Mr. Dean suggested we let Allison come up with most of the answers herself.

With a little help from us, she decided she could start that very day improving her grades; do most of her homework during study hall at school and at the downtown library; try to get a job (Mr. Dean said he would help with that) so she would have her own spending money; get away from home more; quit harping about her hard luck all the time so people would enjoy being with her; try to build her parents up so they would feel better about themselves and about her; be more caring about her teachers and their problems; try to be a friend to her brother instead of a bossy, nagging sister.

We decided that if some of these things worked, Allison wouldn't feel sick so much of the time and wouldn't be so angry.

By the time the session was over, we were all pulling for Allison. That gave her the feeling she has a few friends anyway. I even decided I like her some after all.

This is a good example of something we talk about in Human Behavior class. All of us play different roles at different times: child, parent, and adult. Allison acts like a child most of the time, and so do her parents. That's why she has some of her problems. We members of the group are acting like parents to her. That's okay for now, since her own mom and dad don't act like very good parents. At the same time, we are trying to help Allison to act more grown-up. That is what good parents are supposed to do.

I guess the reason we group members feel good about the whole thing is that Allison's case answers one of our needs too. Not only does a person need parenting but to play the role of parent too. Helping someone else is as important as being helped.

Allison's case gave me a few ideas about how I can do a better job with some of my own problems that have to do with my parents' complaints, like not spending so much time on sports and more time on studying. Miserable thought! Oh well, my parents are going to love it.

Something to Solve

Our assignment for Mr. R.'s class? You guessed it. Choose one big troublesome problem we are faced with right now. List the pluses and the minuses in connection with it. List steps we can take in an attempt to solve or handle the problem. Be ready to report the results either orally or in writing by next week.

Sigh! If I didn't have a problem already, I have one now.

16

Do You Want Me to Be Backward or Not?

It doesn't make too much sense how my parents see things sometimes. For instance, they get really uptight when I show signs of being slow in school. On the other hand, they would like for me to be backward when it comes to acting like other kids my age.

I guess all parents talk a lot about how things were when they were young. They cluck and groan when those sex scenes come on TV and when they listen to the words of rock-group songs. One thing that really gets to them is the talk about birth control for kids. Making condoms available at school, for instance.

My mom said, "When I was in junior high, the thought of having intercourse never even crossed our minds." (I'd guess it crossed their minds a few times.)

I said, "All the noise about condoms doesn't mean we're *all* having sex."

"Well, I'd hope not!" my dad shouted.

"Nevertheless, it's the seal of approval," Mom said, shaking her head.

I figure they were dying to ask me if I'd ever considered having sex with a girl but were afraid I'd either lie or say yes. Either way they'd have a stroke.

In any case, they want me to get ahead in school and in sports, but they want me to stay behind in things like boy-girl stuff, smoking, drinking, using drugs, gabbing on the phone, staying out late, using raunchy language, wearing my hair like other teenagers....

Mostly, I don't mind lagging in those areas. I'm not dying to burn my lungs out smoking, and besides it would slow me down in running and swimming and basketball.

Since a bunch of kids got drunk at one of our parties, and we got hauled down to the police station until our parents bailed us out, I've decided alcohol's not all that great. I thought I was going to be campused until age twenty-one, but my parents finally got over the shock and turned me loose on "good behavior."

My parents aren't the only ones unstrung over teenage drinking. The whole community zeroed in on that after several high-school kids were killed or hurt in drinking accidents. Just one funeral of that sort convinced me drinking's not all that macho.

Besides, some of my friends have alcoholic parents, and their family life is hell. I'm secretly glad adults are doing something about teens' use of alcohol. Our county is considering a law that our driver's license can be temporarily revoked if we are caught DUI. I'm not old enough to get a license yet, but if one thing will make me feel grown-up, it will be that.

About the music and the language and the dress and the hairdos: You practically have to be like people in your age group. Our parents are like other grown-ups, and some of the outfits they wear and the things they do strike us kids as weird.

It's all a matter of when you were born, I guess. Come to think about it, every generation is probably less shocked than the one before.

Take my mom and her mother, for instance. My grandma thinks it's a disgrace that Mom watches talk shows on TV. "How can you stand that junk?" Grandma asks. "Everybody seems to be hung up on sex nowadays."

My mom's answer to that is: "People of your generation were probably hung up on sex, too. It's just that nowadays people discuss it more freely."

It's hard for me to think of Grammy Farnham hung up on sex, or my mom either, for that matter.

Now you won't believe this, but I have to admit some things about modern life really embarrass me. For instance, the school nurse gets kids together to talk about AIDS and birth control. That I can handle. But when she used a banana to show us the correct way to put a condom on, I felt like laughing, but at the same time, I wanted to slip out of the room. I didn't have the nerve to look around and see how the others were taking it, but the kid in front of me scrunched down in his seat.

My parents would be overjoyed if they knew I'm a slow learner when it comes to sex. The thought of being in the midst of a hot sex scene and having to stop long enough to whip out a condom and take time to use it properly turns me off.

For the time being, I don't want to be a daddy, I don't want AIDS or any other STD, and I'm not even crazy about being a stud! Just some kissing and cuddling will do for now.

Something to Discuss with Parents

In one of our group counseling sessions, Mr. Dean asked us how our beliefs about sex are different from what our parents believe. Most of us admitted we don't do much talking about stuff like that with our parents. It's even more embarrassing for them than for us. Still, some parents I know of help their kids plan how to have safe sex if they're going to have it at all. I don't think my parents are quite ready for that. They're pretty slow in some areas. Still, I might give it a try. Talk with them about it, that is.

Something to Do in Class

Mr. Rickman decided to do something to measure our attitudes. He wanted to find out how we feel about sexual intercourse among our age group. He said for those who think it's okay for middle-school students to have sex to go to one end of the room, those who think it's not okay to go to the other end of the room, and those who aren't sure how they feel about it to stand in the middle. I was expecting that most of the kids would settle for the thinking-it's-okay choice, so I was surprised when most of them went to the other end of the line. A few thought it was okay, and quite a few haven't made up their minds, but the largest group was at the it's-not-okay end. Of course, they might not have been telling the truth, but usually kids our age aren't bashful about expressing our opinions. I was one of the not-okay voters, so I was glad to have plenty of company.

17

It's How You Say It That Counts

I couldn't believe it was Shannon's voice on the phone. Sure, girls call boys up all the time, but I'm not one of the ones who get called, except once in a while when some girl wants to know about an assignment or swimming practice — something like that.

Anyway, this beautiful, soft voice said, "Kirk, this is Shannon."

"Oh, hello." My voice came out in a high, nervous squeak.

"I just want to tell you I feel bad about John," Shannon said.

"Yeah, me too," I said, not wanting to talk about John.

The voice went on, still soft and gentle. "I'm sorry about the way I flared up on the date that evening. I didn't know...."

"It's okay," I cut in. This was my frantic voice, but at least it was down an octave or two.

"What I want to say is, I hope you and I can still be friends."

"Well, sure." I was wondering how we were going to go about being friends, living across town from each other, and her in high school and me in middle school. I soon found out.

"Kirk, I'm calling to tell you I just got my driver's license."

"Great," I said in my croaky voice, thinking I couldn't even get a learner's permit until next fall.

"I thought you and I could celebrate by going for a little spin."

"Hey neat. Any old time."

"Like when?" Now Shannon's voice was what you could call businesslike.

By this time, I didn't know exactly how I was feeling. I thought about some of the old sayings that describe how you feel when something's too good to be true: walking on air, on cloud nine, about to burst with joy. Naturally I was feeling all of those things. By the way, I wonder what's different about cloud nine from other clouds.

Anyway, Shannon's voice brought me down off cloud nine. "You name it."

"Name it?" I repeated.

By now her voice was sounding edgy. "When you'd like for me to pick you up."

"Oh. Well, any old time I guess."

"You already said that. What time is 'any old time'?"

The telephone I was talking on is on the counter in the kitchen. My mother was busy getting supper, but I caught her glancing in my direction every now and then. I slipped into the broom closet, which is by the counter, and pulled the door as far shut as it would go.

There was this silence at the other end of the line, and I could imagine Shannon's foot tapping away the seconds. Then she sighed and cleared her throat.

"How about this evening?" I said finally. "Like after supper."

She said, "The sooner the better. I'll pick you up around seven-thirty."

"F-f-fine," I said and hung up. So now I had taken up stuttering. I would have liked to stay in the broom closet until my mother went to another room, but it wasn't likely she'd do that.

"A new friend?" my mom asked in her cheerful voice.

"Shannon," I said, trying to sound offhand.

"The girl you double-dated with?" That was Mom's tell-me-more tone followed by fourteen question marks.

"Yeah. She wanted to say she felt bad about John dying." Why does my voice always crack when John's name comes up?

I edged toward the door to the hall. Mom's voice pattered along behind me. "That was nice of her. Are you going to be seeing her?"

"She just got her driver's license. Wants to take me for a ride." Why did that sound so dumb, I wondered.

"Why you?" Mom asked. Did her voice have to come down so hard on the *you*? As if there's no reason a girl would have any interest in me.

"Why not me?" That was my get-off-my-back tone.

"I didn't mean it that way," Mom said, this time like apologizing. "If I were a girl, you're just the person I'd want to go riding with."

That turned me off, the thought of my mom a teenage girl, but I gave a weak laugh and said, "Thanks." When we worked on this chapter, Miss Hambrick said we could call that my I-don't-really-mean-it-but-I'd-better-say-it tone.

Mom went on in her explaining voice, "What I really meant was, why someone from your school instead of someone from high school? Surely...."

"I know what you're thinking," I said. "What would a glamorous high-schooler see in me?"

As a matter of fact, that's what I was wondering too.

Shannon shed a little light on that later on while we were rodding around town showing off her red convertible—a birthday gift from her grandfather.

A car for a birthday gift? That was definitely out of my league.

Shannon had to be home by nine, so there wasn't much time for us to "become friends." While we were parked in front of my house, though, she said, "Kirk, I'd like to see a lot more of you." Right away she began to giggle. "Not more of *you*—your bod, that is...."

"I know what you mean." I hoped my face wasn't as red as the car.

"What I mean is see you *oftener*." Shannon's voice was all mixed up with giggles.

"Yeah, me too." I couldn't help adding: "But why me? You must have guys swarming all over you."

"Well, not quite that. But I am a little tired of the high-school scene. The guys all want the same thing. It can be something of a disadvantage to be.... well, attractive."

"I shouldn't think you'd mind a disadvantage like that," I told her.

"What I like about you...." She reached over at that point and touched that hunk of hair that hangs down on my forehead no matter how much goop I put on it. "What I like about you," she said again, "is that you're the kind of guy girls want to take care of, to protect."

"I have a couple of parents doing that," I reminded her. "*Over*doing it, in fact." I could imagine those parents peering out from behind the living-room curtain at that very minute.

Shannon quit smoothing the lock of hair on my forehead. "Well, if you'd rather have your parents—" she began in an okay-for-you tone.

"I wouldn't," I cut in. "I wouldn't."

"So shall we go on seeing each other?" Miss Hambrick suggested that this was a pleading voice.

"I suppose," I said. (Really brilliant.)

Shannon said, "I could pick you up a few times a week after school or in the evening and we could do something."

"Well, sure," I said, feeling glad and helpless at the same time. "After school's not so good though. Swimming practice, basketball, track—stuff like that. Besides, I work at Toughy's Fill-'Er-Up after school and evenings every time I get a chance."

Shannon giggled. "What on earth is Toughy's Fillerup?" Sort of the way you would ask a little kid what a *wabby* is when he means rabbit.

"Just what it says," I told her, none too pleasantly. "A filling station."

"Well, you don't have to snap at me. You'll have to admit Toughy's Fillerup...."

"Forget it," I said. I thumped the steering wheel of the birthday gift and said, "Maybe now that you've got this baby, you can give Toughy a little of your trade."

"As long as it's when you're there," she said in a sort of cooing tone. I thought about kissing her but didn't quite have the nerve. I don't usually have too much trouble kissing girls, but Shannon.... Well, that's different.

So that's how come I'm more or less going with this doll. It doesn't even bother me that everyone, including my parents, is probably wondering why me.

I'm actually relieved about Shannon's rejecting the high-school boys because of their all wanting "the same thing." That means she doesn't expect me to make love to her in a really heavy way. I'd really have a problem with that with someone who's been around quite a bit.

Something to Listen For

I thought Mr. Rickman would consider this chapter too stupid to include in the book. To my surprise, he talked about it in a really thoughtful way.

He said: "Kirk, this chapter is more than just an account of a boy-girl relationship. It's about how tone of voice is as important as what that voice says."

Mrs. Atkins got interested too. She said, "This chapter echoes my philosophy that it's not only what you say that counts, but how you say it."

It was Mrs. Atkins's idea to put the descriptions of the voices in.

Between Mr. Rickman and Mrs. Atkins, we had a whole week's worth of assignments and activities to choose from:

1. Write a paper on voices.

2. Do some role-playing, saying the same things in different tones of voice. Note the listeners' reactions to what is said.

3. Listen to what people say and match it up with how they say it. Do the words you hear say something more than if you simply read them?

4. Mr. Rickman gave us an exercise from a drama class he took when he was in college:

   Say the two words <u>one dollar</u> in different tones of voice so that each one gives a different meaning:

   a. <u>One dollar!</u> Special emphasis on both words. Tone of outrage. How do they have the nerve to charge a whole dollar for this?

   b. One dollar. No emphasis on either word. Thoughtful tone. Let's see, do I want to spend a dollar on this item?

   c. One <u>dollar!</u> Tone of delight. Imagine getting this for only one dollar.

   d. One <u>dollar?</u> Tone of disbelief. Did I hear you right? You mean a dollar?

   e. <u>One</u> dollar? Only one? Great!

   f. <u>One dollar:</u> Mild tone. Same emphasis on both words. Believe it or not, that's exactly what I spent for this.

   g. One dollar. With a sigh and no emphasis on either word: Well, here goes another dollar of my hard-earned cash.

5. We had so much fun with that one that we thought up some phrases of our own. One was:

   a. Go out with me? A simple question: Will you go out with me?

   b. Go <u>out</u> with me? Out where, for Pete's sake?

   c. Go out with <u>me?</u> You mean you'd actually go out with <u>me?</u>

18

I Belong to Me

My parents keep hassling me about going with a girl who's older than I am. I talked to Miss Hambrick about it when we were working on this chapter. "It's not as if there's a big difference in our ages—only two years."

Miss Hambrick nodded. "Go ahead talking. You're doing fine."

So I coughed a couple of times and went on. "We learned in English class that Shakespeare's wife was seven years older than him. Anne Hackaway."

"Hathaway," Miss Hambrick said. "Anne Hathaway."

I could feel my face getting red. "I thought the teacher said 'Hackaway'."

Miss H. put her face down on her arm on the desk and began to laugh. "Hackaway," she said. "I love that."

I was anxious to change the subject. "So okay, we'll correct it."

Miss H. lifted her head and looked at me. "No, no, Kirk. Let's keep this part. Kids will enjoy it."

"I doubt if teachers will," I said.

"Adults have a sense of humor too," she said. "Where's *yours*?"

"I have one, but it's more fun to laugh when the joke's on someone else."

She started laughing again. "Kirk, this is getting better and better."

It seemed to me it was getting worse and worse. "We don't want all this on the tape," I said.

"Oh but we do, we do. This is a good example of what happens to people all the time. One of those streaks of Charlie Brownness. People saying things that come out wrong. Hearing things differently from how they were said."

I was pretty tired of the conversation by this time. "It's about time for the bell. I better get moving."

She nodded and began to laugh again. I started slithering toward the door. As I was leaving the room, I heard her say, "Anne Hackaway."

Mr. Rickman thought the Anne Hackaway story was funny. He let the class spend a whole period talking about boos boos — things we have said or things we've heard on TV or somewhere. By the end of the period I was feeling better. I even told Mrs. Atkins about Anne Hackaway. She said, "Kirk, you actually remembered the woman's name, even if you did hear a couple of letters wrong."

So let's get off the hackaway kick and back to my love affair with an older woman. I've decided I love that gal, Shannon. And she says she loves me. How's that for an ego booster? We've been spending a lot of time together. So what's the problem? It's hard to put into words. What's bothering me is that Shannon wants me too completely. I know that doesn't sound like much of a problem for someone who'd never win a popularity contest with the opposite sex.

Thought about talking to my counselor, Mr. Dean, but I was afraid he'd go into some heavy double talk about Shannon's need to be a mother to me or something dumb like that.

I could imagine Mr. Rickman saying: "This isn't a problem someone else can solve for you, Kirk. Let's look at the outcomes."

If I told any of the guys, they'd just say: "Tell her to get lost. Who needs a girl who acts like a wife anyway?"

My parents? They'd give me a big lecture about how there are plenty of girls, and why build your life around one? Get out and have fun with a lot of girls. (Especially girls your own age.)

Sure, I know there are a lot of girls. But they just aren't Shannon. Their eyes don't tilt up a little bit at the outer corners (the way Miss Hambrick described them), and other girls don't look at me as if they would rather be with me than with anyone else.

It's not that I believe there's only one true mate for everyone. That doesn't make sense because there are more females than males. Besides, if it is true, there are a lot of people not hooking up with the right partners.

It's not even that I think there will never be another girl for me. But for right now, Shannon is the one I want.

Mostly what I like best is being with Shannon. But if I go off with the guys or stay after school to shoot baskets or just go off hiking in the hills by myself, Shannon figures I'm getting tired of her.

I try to explain to her that one person can't be your whole life. Trouble is, I'm afraid of losing her. Suppose I did get up enough nerve to say: "Look, I love you, and I like being with you. But I need to have another part of my life, too, that doesn't have a girl in it."

I think what she would say is: "Then we had better break it off. I can't share you. You have come to mean too much to me."

That isn't all though. I keep not getting around to saying what is bothering me the most. What she really did say the other evening was, "If we broke up, I'd commit suicide."

How's that for something to lug around? What if we do break up, and she does kill herself? How would I live with that? I know what my parents would say: "If she's that possessive, you shouldn't have anything to do with her."

I know that. Trouble is, you can know something and still keep on doing what you want to instead of what you should.

But suppose it is true that Shannon wouldn't want to go on living without me. Anyway, if it is true, there's something wrong. I mean, what if I died? Or what if we quit going together? No two people are together forever unless they happen to die at the same time.

Then there's another problem too. Suppose I start getting tired of having Shannon check up on me all the time. I might get sick of having her accuse me of not loving her if I don't let her in on all my plans. I could get fed up with that sort of thing. Then pretty soon I'd really start hurting her.

Maybe the whole thing is a game. I mean, Mr. Dean says to notice what kind of games people play to get others to do what they want them to. Maybe Shannon pulls this old suicide threat on other guys.

So what do I decide from all this stressing out? I think what it all boils down to is that no one can own anyone else. Everyone just belongs to himself or herself. (I'm not sure my parents will go along with that.) If I can't own Shannon, and Shannon can't own me, then we can't decide what each other is going to do. Besides, I don't want enough power to hold someone else's life or death in my hands. That's something I can't handle.

Maybe next time Shannon pulls the old suicide threat, I'll just act real calm and say: "Shannon, your life belongs to you, not to me. You're the one who has to take care of yourself."

Then I'd ask Mr. Dean to talk to the high-school counselors so they can watch out for Shannon. I know you should never ignore a suicide threat, even when it might be a bluff.

Something to Argue About

In Human Behavior we talk a lot about people owning people. It's natural for parents to think of owning their children. When children are little, parents have to tell them what to do and what not to do. Then as the kids get older, they should be given more and more choices until they can run their own lives.

Mr. Rickman says there's a difference between belonging to someone and being possessed by that person. Some examples are:

Husbands and wives belong to each other but get uptight when they start giving each other orders.

The people of a nation belong to that country, but they want to run it rather than having a dictator tell them what to do.

Our assignment: Give examples of people not getting along because of one or both trying to be in charge of the other's life.

19

Candle-Lighting Time

I asked Miss Hambrick if I have to describe what goes on between Shannon and me for this book. She said: "No, everyone deserves an area of privacy that no else can wade around in. When you write, it's okay to leave something to the reader's imagination."

I was afraid of what the reader's imagination would make of my relationship with Shannon. You'd think going with a girl from high school would make me feel older than I am and more experienced. Instead, it makes me feel younger than I am. This relationship with Shannon isn't quite the way I thought going steady would feel like. Shannon's talk about not being able to do without me is more like owning me than loving me.

I don't know what possessed me to mention this to my mom. Her answer was: "Let's face it. A high-school girl who prefers younger boys is probably neurotic."

So that got me to worrying that maybe Shannon wouldn't be in love with me if she wasn't neurotic. Not exactly flattering.

Maybe that's why I was sort of relieved that my knee was hurting last Friday evening when Shannon wanted me to go to a sock hop with her. When I told her I'd better stay home because my knee was acting up, she sniffed and said, "No wonder, the way you punish it with all those athletics."

After that conversation, another unflattering thought entered my mind. Maybe some of Shannon's being attracted to me is that I *am* younger and therefore easier to boss around and control.

Anyway, Shannon didn't call me again that weekend. On Monday we had two new girls in Human Behavior. New students are often put in that class because there's no textbook, and as Mr. Rickman says, "There's no getting behind in a class like this, because you can start learning about people at any time."

Not like math, for instance, where you have to learn everything step by step.

One of these gals, Danfra, is just another girl. Nothing particularly unusual to mention about her. Doesn't seem to want to be at our school. Doesn't look at people. Not shy exactly. More as if she wishes we weren't there. Doesn't respond when we try to be friendly.

But the other girl, Indy, really lights my candle. (That's what we guys in eighth grade say when a girl turns us on. Lance Mowbry says that sounds more like what a poet would say. He prefers *sparks my engine*. Figures of speech, Mrs. Atkins calls them, phrases that say one thing and mean something else.)

Well, whichever. This Indy was lighting candles and sparking engines all over the place right away.

She isn't tall. Shannon is. Almost as tall as me, in fact, when she wears high heels. Indy's not glamorous like Shannon. Not even beautiful. Cute looking though. Her hair is short and turns up a little at the ends, so it sticks out away from her face. A "feather cut," Miss Hambrick calls it. Whatever it is, I dig it. Her eyes are brown—not dark brown—more the color of syrup. Miss Hambrick says, "Amber, perhaps?" Indy has a really friendly smile and tiny little specks of freckles sprinkled around on the top of her nose and below her eyes.

Monday turned out to be a good day. Not just on account of the new students, but because of a talk Mrs. Atkins and I had during study hall when she was helping me with the spelling and sentences of one of my chapters.

She said, "Kirk, I like your writing."

"You *do?*" I couldn't believe a teacher, especially one who teaches English, could think it was any good.

"I like it because it's clear and not complicated. You say what you mean, and the way you say it reflects you, the author. Your writing is simple."

I nodded. "You've got that right. That's what's wrong with it."

Mrs. Atkins laughed. "I don't mean simple like in simpleminded. Some of the best authors write simply. Here, let me give you an example."

She got a book off one of the shelves. "*The Prophet*," she said. "One of my favorites. This author, Kahlil Gibran, uses short sentences and short words, but what he writes comes across like poetry. Listen to this. It's a passage about children. Here's what the prophet says to his audience":

(I turned my tape recorder on so the quotation would be exactly the way it was written.)

"Your children are not your children," she read.

Mrs. Atkins glanced up from the book. "That's the author's message," she explained. "I'll skip the next few lines. Here we are; this is the part I like best:

> You may give them your love but not your thoughts,
> For they have their own thoughts.
> You may house their bodies but not their souls,
> For their souls dwell in the house of tomorrow, which you cannot visit, not even in your dreams.
> You may strive to be like them, but seek not to make them like you.

"Hey, all right," I said. "You say the guy's a real writer?"

Mrs. Atkins nodded. "A first-class one. A Lebanese poet, author, and artist who died in our country in 1931. I read somewhere that Gibran spent ten years writing this book, and as you can see, it's very short."

"Ten years! He should have had Miss Hambrick on his case."

Mrs. Atkins went on to say she had chosen the passage she read to me because it says much the same thing as my chapter, "I Belong to Me."

"Thanks," I said, thinking how much Mrs. Atkins knows about how to make kids feel okay about themselves.

I don't have to have second sight to guess that one of Mrs. Atkins's assignments will be to read *The Prophet* to see what different authors' writing styles are like. "Such a clear message and such short, simple sentences," I can hear her saying.

20

If Only the Floor Would Open and Swallow Me Up!

Even if I am beginning to have some doubts about Shannon, being her boyfriend gives me some confidence around other girls. At least, that's what I thought. I decided to use some of that confidence with the new girl, Indy, who is in Human Behavior and also my English class. I figured I'd better not waste any time, especially as our school makes a big point of making newcomers feel welcome.

It's pretty awkward in middle school asking someone for a date, partly on account of transportation. Most of our dating is in groups: shows, sports events, parties, stuff like that. We usually meet somewhere or go by bus or walk or get hauled somewhere by our parents (quite embarrassing).

Besides, I wasn't about to ask Indy for a date and risk getting turned down. An offer of help seemed like the best gamble. So on the way out of English class on Indy's third day at our school, I caught up with her and said, "In case you'd like some help getting caught up in this class...uh...I'd be glad...."

She gave me a friendly smile and said, "Thanks, but Mrs. Atkins gave me a copy of what's gone on so far, and several kids have offered to help me."

"Well, thanks," I said. "I mean—"

What did I mean? I wasn't supposed to be thanking her; it was the other way around, and she had already said thanks.

All I had in mind was to bound off down the hall and get out of her sight as fast as possible.

"There is something though," she said.

I stopped and held my breath for the next five minutes or so until she got around to telling me what the "something" was. "Mrs. Atkins did tell me you are working on some kind of writing project, and you might be able to fill me in on some things about the school."

"Anything!" I practically yelled. "Anything," I added in a calmer tone. That still sounded pretty bold, I decided. Something she could really take wrong. "That is...," I began.

"Maybe we could get together this evening or sometime and get acquainted," she suggested.

"Hey, super. How about if I have my dad bring me by to pick you up this evening and we could go to the library?"

"No point in going to the library," Indy said. "You could just come by my house — 1204 Maple — and we could visit there."

"Sounds great. You're only a few blocks from where I live. I can ride over on my bike. About six-thirty?"

"Make it seven, and bring your notebook."

It was a relief to be able to tell my parents I was going to a classmate's house to study instead of to a party or somewhere with Shannon.

They might not have been quite as pleased as I was to discover Indy's parents weren't home for the evening. The perfect setting, I thought, to act the way a guy is supposed to act with a candle-lighting type of girl on a get-acquainted date. Maybe I could finally match some of the locker-room stories of my buds. Not that I believed all of them, but up to this point, I hadn't even been able to think up a convincing lie.

Indy evidently expected more than just a study session, I decided, or she wouldn't have invited me on an evening when her parents weren't home. That's what gave me the nerve to put my hand up under her T-shirt while we were studying my notes on short-story writing.

Indy sat up straight, and her body stiffened so suddenly that she was a different person with no warning. Naturally I pulled my hand out of the T-shirt, getting my watch caught on the top of her skirt in the process.

Please, Lord, I thought, if the world is going to end, let it be now.

"Do you happen to read the newspapers and watch the newscasts on TV?" Indy asked in an ice-cold voice.

"Well, sure," I said. (I don't actually spend much time that way.)

"Then you've heard quite a bit about date rape and sexual harrassment," Indy went on in the same icicle voice.

"Rape!" I shouted. "Sexual...!"

"Harrassment," she finished for me. "Like when guys think they can get by with anything they want to with us dumb girls."

What could I have said? I thought later of several clever things, but all that came out of my mouth at that minute was, "I thought...."

She said, "Well, next time don't think; just ask."

"I guess I'd better go," I said.

"I guess," she agreed, handing me my jacket and walking me to the door.

I felt so bummed I couldn't go to sleep that night, and my stomach was giving me fits the next morning at the thought of facing Indy. I don't know what I expected, but I was surprised she didn't glare at me or act as if anything had happened. Just came over and laid my notebook on my desk. "You forgot this," she said.

Miss Hambrick kept asking me what was wrong. "You're just not with it today, Kirk. Anything you want to talk about?"

Finally I told her about my big evening with Indy. She just nodded as if there wasn't anything very shocking about the episode.

"This is definitely not something we want in the book," I said.

"Maybe we do," she said. "Maybe it's important. It might help to explain why sexual activity is moving down into the grade schools. Perhaps boys and girls figure it's expected of them. TV tells them so. Our permissive society tells them so. Magazines and newspapers tell them so. Maybe it takes an Indy to tell them it isn't necessarily so."

"But Indy wouldn't want it in the book," I said.

"We wouldn't have to use her name. Anyway, we'll ask her."

Before I had a chance to protest that idea, Miss Hambrick and Indy and I were in the office where we work on this book, and Miss Hambrick was explaining to Indy about the project.

"Hey, neat!" Indy said. Then she looked at us as if she was wondering why she was there. Miss H. told her about what she and I had been discussing. "Indy, how would you feel about what happened yesterday evening being in the book?"

Indy frowned and thought about it for a while. Finally she said: "Sure. Go ahead. I don't mind going on record with what I said."

Miss Hambrick hugged her. "Good girl. Now if I can convince Kirk to go on record with what he *did*."

"Started to do," Indy said. "He didn't get very far."

"Not as far as most of the guys are going nowadays," I put in. "At least what they claim."

Indy sighed. "Anyway, it was probably a typical scene. And mind you, it's not that I don't like boys. I do. A lot. But that doesn't mean—well, you know what."

She actually smiled at me as she flounced out of the office. (I think *flounced* is what she did. That's a word they use in books quite a bit.)

Something to Share with No One but Yourself

Our next assignment for Human Behavior was strange. Mr. R. told us to write a paper—an "essay," he called it—that no one was to read except the person who wrote it.

"How will you know we wrote it?" Rusty asked.

"It's not important for me to know. It's important for you to know whether you write it or not."

"But how can you give us a grade?" Sophie asked.

"I can't. You give yourself a grade. Whatever you think it's worth."

"You mean—" Lance began.

"I mean get to work. Now here's what this assignment is to tell *you*: What is your philosophy about sexual activity between males and females? When should it begin? Whom should it be between? What should the circumstances be? How private should it be? What kind of precautions should be taken? What is your opinion of the way sex is portrayed on TV? Anything you want to write on the subject."

"But if nobody's to read it...." I said.

His answer was: "The purpose of the assignment is to make you examine your own beliefs and your own sexual behavior, not just what you are being told by others. Be tough on yourself, okay?"

I'm not sure yet just what my essay will say. One thing I'm sure of, though, the scene between Indy and me isn't going to be one of my stories for the locker room.

21

All She Said Was...

I mentioned that two new gals came into our Human Behavior class one day. After the bad scene with Indy, it occurred to me that the other girl, Danfra, counts too. Usually new kids cause quite a stir. Depends on what they look like, if they're good at sports, but most of all, do they seem like the rest of us? In other words, do they fit in?

At our school we go all out to welcome newcomers. That's one of our specialties. We're like a small community, you might say. No longer those babies from grade school, but not those bottom-of-the-heap freshmen at high school. (Not yet!)

Quite often new students are put in Mr. Rickman's Human Behavior class because that's a good way for them to gain some understanding about themselves and not feel as self-conscious as new students usually do.

I already mentioned that Danfra didn't fit right in. Sort of like a jigsaw-puzzle piece in the wrong box. (Mrs. Atkins says that's a figure of speech—saying something that means something else. Mrs. A. loves figures of speech.)

It's hard to describe just how Danfra's different. Looks ordinary enough: straight brown hair, kind of pale skin, small compared to other eighth-graders, straight black eyebrows that are like a couple of hyphens. (Another figure of speech.) She doesn't dress like the rest of us. Of course, that doesn't matter nowadays when you can wear any old thing and get away with it.

My parents are always asking why kids want to look so shabby—shredded denims, shoes without laces, patches all over. I try to explain that our clothes aren't shabby; they're just *in*.

What doesn't make sense is that I think Danfra's outfits *do* look shabby. Most girls our age wear dresses that are really short or really long or else they wear tops and jeans or skirts. Danfra wears a longish dress that looks as if it should be on someone else. Someone older. I mean, the top part — the waist — hits her down below the hips, and the sleeves are too long. Maybe her clothes aren't all like that. After all, she's been here only a week, and she has worn the same dress and tacky sweater every day.

What makes you keep looking at her isn't her clothes. It's her pale gray eyes. Somehow you expect them to be dark on account of those black eyebrows. It's not the color of her eyes that makes me stare at her, though. It's that when she looks at me, I feel as if she's looking inside of me or through me. As if she's reading me. At the same time, it's like she's miles away. Just someone not there. I keep wanting to look behind me to see if she's staring at someone else.

Well, I did a lousy job with that description. The problem is, I had to hand it in for English class. When Mrs. Atkins went over the paper with me, she said: "Kirk, you have made me curious about Danfra. Could you get acquainted with her and then try again to describe her?"

By that time I was curious myself. So I tried to start a conversation with Danfra on the way out of class one day. It was plain she didn't want to talk to me. Just looked straight ahead as we walked along and answered my questions with a word or two. By the time we got to her locker, I was the one feeling self-conscious and rejected.

"Don't give up on people," our counselor, Mr. Dean, is always telling us. "Give up on some things but not on a person."

So all right. I'd find out about this offbeat girl yet.

The next day after class I caught up with her in the hall and said, "Hi." My voice came out louder than I'd meant for it to, and it sounded cracky like when your voice is changing.

"Hello," she said, looking through my head with those pale gray eyes.

"I'm a reporter for our school newspaper," I said, "and I'm supposed to do a write-up on new students to the school." (That was a lie — we don't even have a school newspaper yet — but I decided honesty isn't necessarily the best policy right now.)

She just looked at me — or into me — and waited for me to go on.

Before she had a chance to look away, I whipped a paper out of my notebook and handed it to her. "I made out this questionnaire for you to fill out."

She said, "Oh," and stuffed the paper into the pocket of the saggy, black sweater that looked as if it would fall off her shoulders at any minute. I felt like a seven-year-old talking to an adult. "Do you think you could fill it in and get it back to me by tomorrow?"

"If they're questions I can answer," she said.

"Thanks a lot," I said. What in heck was I thanking her for? I'd never see that questionnaire again. I did though. The next day. "Here," she said, thrusting it at me. I found myself looking forward to reading it but was frankly disappointed when I did. Here's what it amounted to:

Question: Why did you move to our town?
Answer: We travel a lot.

Question: Where do you live?
Answer: No permanent address yet. Still looking for the ideal place.

Question: Who's in your family?
Answer: My parents, three brothers.

Question: What does your dad do for a living?
Answer: Top-secret job.

Question: Does your mother work or stay home?
Answer: Goes to work every day.

Question: Where did you live before you came here?
Answer: We travel a lot.

Question: What does your family do for fun?
Answer: Hike a lot. Read. Have lots of people around us all the time.

Question: Where did you get the name *Danfra*?
Answer: Named after my father, whose name ~~was~~ is Dan Fred.

(I was sort of puzzled that she had crossed out the word *was*.)

Question: Do you have a nickname?
Answer: No.

Question: Would you like to come to my house after school some day?
Answer: Can't promise anything. We'll be moving any day.

I told Mrs. Atkins I didn't feel as if I knew Danfra any better than before she filled out the paper. I explained that I had left spaces after each question so she'd have plenty of room to write a bunch of stuff.

Mrs. Atkins said: "Maybe it's because your interview questions ask for simple information. There's nothing about feelings; likes and dislikes; wishes; disappointments."

"Gad, I'd never know how to ask that sort of stuff," I said.

"Maybe you need to talk to Danfra to find out 'that sort of stuff.' Find out what's written between the lines."

Sigh! Finding out about Danfra is like reading print that's all blurred. I wish she'd kept on traveling and not landed in our town.

Something to Imagine

Mrs. Atkins played a tape of the Simon and Garfunkel song "The Sounds of Silence" in English class. She said, "What we don't say can be more important than what we do say." She told us to pretend we are interviewing someone who doesn't want to be interviewed. "Make up the conversation as it might take place," she said, "then fill in some things you think the person you are interviewing might be leaving out."

We all groaned. Trying to figure out what people don't say is out of our realm.

Mrs. Atkins told me privately that instead of that assignment she'd like for me to try to find out some things Danfra might have told me and didn't. Since Danfra isn't in that English class, she wouldn't know I'm trying to pry more information out of her in order to carry out an assignment.

I'm tempted to just go ahead and flunk this one. Knowing more about Danfra isn't one of my burning desires.

22

Home Must Be Somewhere

I didn't know how to approach Danfra about getting more information so I just jumped in with both feet. On the way out of Human Behavior the next morning I caught up with her and said: "I lied to you about the questionnaire. I don't work on the school paper. In fact, there isn't one."

"That makes us even," she said. "I lied on the questionnaire. At least I didn't tell it like it is."

"I would like to know you better," I said. By this time we were walking down the hall, and she was several steps ahead of me, which tells you something.

"So give me the stupid paper back and I'll fill in what I didn't say. Then we'll see whether you want to know me better or not."

I scrambled through my notebook until I finally found the questionnaire and gave it to her. By the time I had picked up the junk that had fallen out of my notebook, Danfra was way down the hall, and I didn't see her again until the next morning.

"Here." She pushed the questionnaire at me and hurried to her desk. All day I was curious to see what she had written, but I didn't have a chance to read it until after supper. This time it read like this (just what had been there in the first place, plus what she added):

Question: Why did you move to our town?
Answer: We travel a lot. From town to town, street to street, house to house.

Question: Where do you live?
Answer: No permanent address yet. Still looking for the ideal place. *Any* place, that is. Right now it's a big broken house where lots of families hang out.

Question: Who's in your family?
Answer: My parents, three brothers. *One* parent, that is. My mom. One brother with us and two others in foster homes. Unless they're in jail by now.

Question: What does your dad do for a living?
Answer: Top-secret job. Everything about him is top secret. Who he is, where he is. *If* he is.

Question: Does your mother work or stay home?
Answer: Goes to work every day. *Looks* for work every day. No one's dying to hire someone who dresses like a bag lady and has no skills and no permanent address and no car to get to work in.

Question: Where did you live before you came here?
Answer: We travel a lot. Like from one ghetto to another, trying to find one that isn't gang infested and rat infested.

Question: What does your family do for fun?
Answer: Hike a lot. Read. Have lots of people around us all the time. Hike everywhere we go. The closest we ever came to a car was an old pickup Mom's live-in took off in after my brother Aaron was born. Read? Every want ad in every newspaper we find in trash cans and on park benches and anywhere else. About the people.... There are always more people than room for them in the shelters. Enough people to last me for the rest of my life.

Question: Where did you get the name *Danfra*?
Answer: Named after my father, whose name ~~was~~ is Dan Fred. I don't know who my father was, and I doubt if my mother does. Could have been Bill or Harry or any old name. But it wasn't *Dan* or *Fred*. So where did my mother get that name? Who knows? Probably from one of her daydreams.

Question: Do you have a nickname?
Answer: No. People have to know you before they give you a nickname. They have to think of you as a person.

Question: Would you like to come to my house after school some day?
Answer: Can't promise anything. We'll be moving any day. Can't promise anything except that I never go to people's houses. And it is true that we'll be moving any day. You're allowed only so much time at any one shelter.

I just sat and stared at the questionnaire, wishing I had never given it to Danfra in the first place. One thing I noticed about Danfra's answers was that they sounded almost as if they were written by a regular author instead of a school kid. I wished I could write like that. Some of her answers were kind of like poetry that doesn't rhyme. A little like *The Prophet.*

I dreaded to see Danfra the next day, and I'm sure she felt the same about it. She didn't look at me all first period. I followed her out of the room and said, "Do you mind if I call you Danny?"

Her head jerked around, and for once she looked straight at me—not through me or past me, but *at* me. "If that's what you want," she said, and started on down the hall ahead of me.

"That's not all I want," I said.

She turned around and looked at me again. "No?"

"I want to walk home with you after school today."

"Why?" She looked ahead and went on walking.

"Danfra. Danny. Does a guy have to have a reason to want to walk home with a girl?"

"Yes." That was a simple enough answer.

"Well then, because I want to know you better."

She said, "I should think the questionnaire would accomplish that."

"Well, it didn't. Knowing *about* you isn't the same as knowing *you.*

She shrugged. "Okay. I'll be at the front door of the building after school in case you haven't changed your mind."

I bumbled my way through the next five periods wondering what had possessed me to decide to get myself involved in Danfra's life. This was one of those "if onlys" we had talked about in class. Well, with any luck, Danfra wouldn't follow through on her promise.

She did though. And the next day I wrote about it for the following chapter in my book.

23

This Is Home?

It seemed that Danfra and I walked miles. Actually I do a lot of walking, up in the hills besides in town, but this walk had an endlessness about it, like walking in a dream and never getting anywhere.

Partly, it wasn't how far we went as much as that we didn't talk. Walking by yourself is one thing, but I felt really uncomfortable clipping along beside Danfra as if we didn't know each other. The truth is, we didn't.

Finally we went down under a bridge. Danfra waved her hand toward a slope of concrete tucked up under the highway.

"This is where we used to live," she said.

"Here!" I wished my voice hadn't come out so shocked. "Here?" I asked in my regular voice.

She nodded.

"Where did you move to?"

I wanted her to say, "Into a house," but what she said was: "To a shelter. A lot of shelters. One after another."

"That beats this, I guess," I said.

"I liked this better."

"Why didn't you stay here?"

"The police wouldn't let us. Said it wasn't safe." Danfra laughed, but not the kind of laugh when something's funny.

"It's probably good they made you move," I said.

"I'd rather be here, but the people at Social Services wouldn't let Mom keep us kids if we stayed here."

"Why did you like it better here?"

Danfra was looking at her former home with those eyes that look as if they're seeing something that isn't there.

She said, "We had bedrolls, so it wasn't too cold at night. Sort of, though. Mom likes to collect boxes, so we each had one. A box for her, a box for my stuff, and a box for Aaron's. Aaron's my brother. He's eleven." Danfra's voice was soft when she mentioned her brother, as if she was telling herself something, and she was almost smiling a little.

"We also had a wooden crate," Danfra went on, "where we kept the food we scrounged and toothpaste and stuff like that. My mom even kept a picture of Aaron and me there. We also had a big box for our clothes."

No wonder her clothes looked as if they belonged to someone else; they had.

"Where did you get water?" I suddenly realized this was a real interview. The kind Mrs. Atkins had in mind.

Danfra pointed to a thin little stream trickling along below the bridge.

"Isn't it more comfortable at the shelter — shelters?" I could imagine myself taking notes like a real reporter. I didn't need a notebook though. Danfra's story was writing itself in my brain.

Danfra looked at me — through me — and said, "I don't want to talk about it anymore."

"That's okay," I told her. I knew a real reporter would squeeze some more information out of her. All of a sudden I didn't want to be a real reporter. "I'll walk you home," I said.

That sounded dumb under the circumstances, but it's one of those things you can't erase once your voice has said it.

Danfra didn't bother to answer. Just started walking, and I tagged along even though I figured she didn't want me to.

"Couldn't you ride the bus to school?" I asked, rushing to keep up with her.

"No way," she said.

For once, I knew how she felt. School buses meant people asking questions and trying to get acquainted. Or making fun of someone who was different.

After a while we came to a beaten-up brick building. We went inside and through a kind of lobby where a bunch of little kids were looking at books and playing with toys.

I followed Danfra up two flights of rickety stairs to a long room where there were a lot of cots lined up against the wall.

"Our address is cots numbers five, six, and seven," Danfra said in a sour tone. "My mom's out looking for a job, but Aaron's here. He won't play with the other kids. Aaron will never, ever admit being like...." Danfra stared off into space. "Like we are," she said finally.

"I hope not," I said.

Danfra turned and stared at me. Right *at* me. I had the feeling she was listening to me too.

"Why did you say that?" she asked. She sounded angry.

I was also wondering why I had said it. I stuttered around trying to find a good answer. "I just meant if Aaron can't accept ... accept who he is, he might change things."

Danfra kept staring at me as if she expected me to say something else.

"Kids do grow up, you know," I said.

Danfra actually smiled. It occurred to me it was the first time I had seen her really smile.

"I'll introduce you to Aaron." Danfra headed toward cot number seven. "This is Aaron," she said, "and this is Kirk, a boy from school."

"Hi, partner," I said. I knew right away it was the wrong thing to have said. It didn't sound real, and Aaron knew it didn't. He just sat there straight as a soldier with his chin up high and his lips closed together in a straight line. It was as if he couldn't let his body relax or his chin drop or his lips open. If he did, he would crumple up and start to cry.

I wanted to do something about that eleven-year-old kid, and I knew I couldn't. Nothing that would last.

I had said, "Kids do grow up." Now I thought this kid—this eleven-year-old—already had.

"I'd better get home," I said, and right away I wished I hadn't used the word *home*. "My folks will think I've been kidnapped," I added with a wimpy laugh. I wished I hadn't said *kidnapped*. Being kidnapped probably sounded like *so what* to Danfra and Aaron.

Danfra walked to the top of the stairs with me. "Thanks," she said.

"What for?"

"For treating me like a someone."

"You are," I said. I stood there looking stupid.

Danfra gave me that look that said she expected me to say something else.

Finally I said, "I was going to write about this, about you, that is, for a chapter in my book."

"What's stopping you?"

"Of course, I won't. Write it, that is. It's too personal. Like I waded around in your private life."

"Write it," she said, "and use our names. Tell it like it is."

Surely she was being sarcastic. I looked at her, and she was looking at me as if we had connected.

"You mean it?" I asked.

"I do. And be sure to say what you did, that kids grow up. Right now we're trapped in childhood, but it's not forever."

Miss Hambrick agreed with me, that's the perfect ending for this chapter. Children are trapped in childhood, but it doesn't have to be forever.

Something to Risk

Mrs. Atkins was so impressed with the story about Danfra and Aaron that she urged the kids in the class to take a risk and interview some of the so-called losers at our school. "Promise not to use their real names unless they want you to," she reminded us. "Then write a paper or tell the class about the result. Were you rebuffed and told to mind your own business? Did you make a new friend? Did you change your opinion about the person you chose for the interview? Did this interview cause you to see things in a different light?

I added my brilliant advice: "Go for it!"

24

Your Moccasins Hurt My Feet

I lay awake part of that night thinking about Danfra and Aaron and wondering if I could do anything about them. Just be friends, I decided. You can't change the world, Mr. Rickman had said. I knew I couldn't change Danfra's world.

The next morning in Human Behavior I kept watching the door, ready to smile and wave when Danfra came in. When she hadn't shown up by the time the second bell rang, I knew she wasn't going to. Danfra wouldn't walk into class late, I figured. That would be giving people a chance to look at her. Danfra's trick is to melt out of sight as much as possible.

I was so busy thinking about Danfra and her family, including the mother I hadn't met, the brothers in foster homes, and the top-secret father, that I hardly noticed Indy following me down the hall after class.

"Hey, Kirk," she said.

I turned around. "Oh, hi." My voice must have sounded cautious. She laughed.

"What's funny?" I asked.

"You," she said. "Nice-funny."

"What does nice-funny mean?" I asked.

"The way you act so unsure of yourself. As if you're worried about how you're coming across."

"I have good reason to be," I reminded her. "You should know that."

"Forget about that evening. I'm ready to start over. Not that same way though."

"What did you have in mind?" I asked, trying to sound sure of myself.

"Another study session maybe. *Study*, that is."

"Sure. What else?" Right away I realized how that sounded and began to bumble my way out of it. "I don't mean what else *besides* study. That is, in *addition* to study. I mean *instead* of study—"

She giggled. "I know what you mean."

"I didn't think you'd ever speak to me again after that night."

She smiled that friendly smile at me. "I can't resist that blond-hair, brown-eyes combination. To say nothing of the dimple in your chin."

I could feel my face getting red. "Do you have to call it a dimple?"

"Is there a better word?"

"Dent maybe?"

She giggled again. "Okay. Dent. Or cleft. That's what they call it in stories. By the way, here's my next class. See you."

She ducked into the door of the classroom.

I put my finger against the hole in my chin. The dimple I had hated all my life. The dimple my mother had loved all my life. Women were strange, I thought. Anyway, I was glad there was something about me they couldn't resist.

The scene with Indy practically erased everything else in my mind for the rest of the school day. By the time school was out, I got this feeling I'd had first period of something not just right. Then I remembered. Danfra hadn't come to school. Not to first class anyway.

I stopped by the office and asked one of the secretaries if Danfra Blakeslee had been at school that day. She looked at the attendance list. "Nope. Absent all day."

I had planned to go to the gym to shoot a few baskets but found myself on my skateboard headed toward Danfra's shelter.

When I got there and started up the rickety stairs, a woman came out of an office and asked where I was going.

"I need to see the Blakeslees on third floor."

"Not here anymore," the woman said. "Left last night."

"Do you know where they went?"

She shrugged. "Someone in a station wagon picked them up. Their time at this shelter ran out."

Something heavy was sitting in the middle of my stomach. I was thinking what it would be like if someone came to my house and told the family, "Your time here is up."

"You don't know who it was that picked them up or where they went?" I asked.

The woman shrugged again. "Who knows about these people?" Someone from Social Services, I suppose." She turned away from me and went into the office.

"These people," she had said. I wanted to yell after her: "The Blakeslees aren't 'these people.' They are Danfra and Aaron and their mom, and they are all filled up with hurt."

Danfra had really melted out of sight this time.

First thing next morning I made an appointment to talk with Mr. Rickman during his free period. Thank goodness for Reachout teachers! Sometimes you really need them.

"Kirk, I'm glad you're here," he said when I went into his office. "I thought something was bothering you yesterday and today. As if you were off somewhere else."

"I was." I told him about going to the shelter with Danfra and what I'd found out about her family. "You know something weird happened to me when I saw Aaron," I said.

"Which was...?"

"Which was I felt as if I *was* that kid. As if I was in his skin sitting there so straight like I was made out of wood and all ready to fall apart if I moved."

Mr. R. nodded as if he understood what I was trying to say.

That encouraged me to go on. "I feel sorry for Danfra and worried about her and her mom, but it's different with Aaron. I can feel his feelings."

Mr. R. said: "Kirk, sometimes you say something that's very important. This is one of those times."

"Then you do know what I mean."

"I know exactly. Stop and think how a lot of human problems would be smoothed out if we were able to try on other people's feelings the way we do clothes, to find out how they feel on us. That makes me think of a saying—I can't remember exactly how it goes—but something about if you are to understand someone else, you would have to walk a ways in that person's moccasins."

I liked that. "Well, right now," I said, "I'm walking in Aaron's moccasins, and they pinch like crazy."

I wasn't surprised at Mr. Rickman's next assignment for our class: Imagine you are someone else, someone you know a little but not a lot. Pretend you can discard your own feelings for a little while and substitute the feelings of that person. Describe what it is like to be that person. How does it make you feel?

25

Runningawayness

In some classes we kids try to get the teacher talking as soon as the beginning bell rings. That's to put off getting to work right away. In Human Behavior it doesn't work. Mr. Rickman turns what we say into a problem to figure out. We wind up doing more thinking than if we just read a chapter and answered some questions.

Anyway, our big attempt on Friday was to mention that Bonnie Dunbar, one of our schoolmates, had run away from home.

Mr. Rickman's answer was: "You don't have to leave home to be running away. I don't mean running away from home isn't serious. I meant we do a lot of running away in our everyday lives."

We looked blank, and Rusty said, "Huh?"

"Some of your are running away right now," the teacher went on.

"We are?" Nedra asked.

Mr. R. nodded. "Janelle, for instance. What science-fiction novel are you reading today?"

"Oh ... uh...."

"Never mind," Mr. R. said. "Reading and sleeping during class are minor examples of escaping." He took his grade book out of a drawer in his desk. "Now here is a student in one of my classes who hasn't earned one single grade all semester. Nothing but zeros. I have checked with other teachers, and he is performing—or rather *not* performing—the same way in all classes. Would you call that a kind of running away?"

We started offering reasons for the kid's failure. Maybe he's not very bright. Maybe he hates school. Maybe he's under too much pressure from his parents. Maybe....

"Now you are making alibis for this boy's behavior," Mr. R. pointed out. "An alibi is an excuse for not doing what you are supposed to do. Making alibis is another kind of running away."

"Gee, Mr. Rickman, you make everything sound like a kind of running-awayness," Daren complained.

"Not most things," Mr. R. said. "However, it's alarming how much of our time is spent that way. Let's suppose that running away means not facing up to things the way they really are. Take the boy who is failing all of his subjects. He is what we teachers call a 'psychological' dropout. *Psychological* means having to do with our minds or our feelings. It doesn't have to be actually going away."

"So how is this boy a psycho—whatever you call it—dropout?" Rusty asked.

"He isn't looking at things the way they really are," Mr. Rickman explained. "If he were, he would do one of two things: withdraw from school; or start studying to get some sort of payment, such as grades, for being here."

"Maybe his parents won't let him drop out," Matt suggested.

"Whatever the reason, he's still not dealing with reality," Mr. R. insisted. "He's bugging out, although not in the same way Bonnie did."

It came to my mind that Bonnie might come out better in the long run than the kid who was wasting thirty-five hours a week at school. Bonnie might discover home isn't as bad as she thought it was. Or her folks might get upset enough to understand her problems better. But flunking everything.... Well, that's sort of like sleepwalking your way through the year.

Several of us in the class decided poor grades aren't necessarily a cop-out. It could be a matter of someone's being more interested in other things.

Mr. R. went along with that. "Everyone needs to experience some failure. But *being* a failure is downright destructive. Failure generates more failure."

Margarita said, "Some people don't even try because they are afraid they're going to fail."

"Exactly," Mr. R. agreed. "That's when failure's really a cop-out: when the individual won't take a risk. I suspect that's why the student I mentioned won't attempt any schoolwork."

"Maybe he's telling the adults in his life they can't make him do something he doesn't want to," I suggested.

Mr. R. nodded. "Probably. Trouble is, the kid himself gets punished along with the people he's punishing. Now, besides punk grades, what are some examples of runningawayness?"

Most of our examples were common ones like getting drunk, spacing out on drugs, making excuses, pretending to be someone you're not, being absent a lot from school or work, committing suicide, having a nervous breakdown.

Mr. R. says doctors don't use the term *nervous breakdown* anymore, but mental illness or emotional disturbance can be a form of runningawayness.

He said: "The person doesn't deliberately use mental illness to get out of something. Things just build up and get too big to handle, so the person cracks. That's a cry for help."

We couldn't agree about whether unmarried teenage girls getting pregnant is a runningawayness. Some of the comments were:

"I knew this girl who got pregnant so the guy would marry her so she could get away from her parents. That's running away."

"Some unmarried girls keep their kids and bring them up okay."

"And some keep their kids and then don't take care of them."

"That's not fair to the kid."

"At least it had a chance to be born."

"It's no favor to be born with a bunch of strikes against you."

Mr. R. said, "Now you're talking about consequences, not whether pregnancy out of wedlock is an escape from reality."

We finally concluded it depends on the reason for the pregnancy and the way it is handled.

We talked about sickness sometimes being a cop-out. Ms. McGregor, our school nurse, came to talk to our class about that. She said an illness that is caused by emotions but shows up as physical symptoms is called "psychosomatic." That means the ailment involves both the mind and the body.

That brought a discussion of how sickness is sometimes used to run away from unpleasant situations. This might be consciously, like a mother staging a heart attack every time her daughter threatens to move away from home. Or it could be something the person doesn't consciously bring on.

Ms. McGregor also talked about accident proneness. She said the tendency for a person to have accidents frequently might be a subconscious way of getting attention or getting out of something we don't want to face.

She finished her talk by saying some illnesses and accidents can't be avoided, like when something falls on you or you get strep throat, so these aren't cop-outs. The important thing is to examine our pattern of illnesses and accidents to see whether we're using them as crutches or not.

Mr. R. told us to look back at some of our own experiences when a sickness or an accident might possibly have been psychosomatic. In other words, did our feelings have anything to do with our being sick in order to wriggle out of an unpleasant task or situation?

Come to think of it, that bad knee I had when I didn't want to go to the dance with Shannon: Was it all in my head or all in my knee? Well, whichever. Shannon sulked for two days. At least she didn't threaten suicide.

26

Did It Have to Happen?

Mostly we kids don't pay too much attention to everything adults say to us. They talk on their wavelengths, and we hear on ours.

Ever since John died, though, things grown-ups have said keep coming back to my mind. Like Mrs. Atkins saying if we feel guilty enough, it makes us think we're being punished, so we decide we don't have to do any changing. That's not the way she said it, but that's what I think she had in mind. That set me to thinking. If we paid more attention to what we're doing, we might head off some bad stuff in our lives. I know I'm not saying this well, but Miss Hambrick says let it pour out. "You need to hear yourself thinking," is the way she put it.

People work hard and spend a lot of money at trying to keep from getting sick. Maybe we should look ahead more and try to figure out some ways to prevent bad things from happening.

I remember that in one of our counseling sessions Mr. Dean said grief is an illness, and it takes a long time to get well from it.

Could we ward off some of our grief the way we do some sicknesses?

Talking about that reminds me of something John's mother said when she was trying to make me feel less guilty after John died. She mentioned that John and I made some bad choices. I think she was trying to say we weren't bad kids.

Mr. Rickman must have been reading my mind lately, or else he was thinking some of the same things I was. John was killed on Wednesday of If-Only Week. How's that for something strange?

On the next Monday Mr. R. said, "Our If-Only Week is over, but it's something I hope you will carry along and think about when you make grave decisions."

The class was really quiet, knowing this was building up to something heavy.

Mr. R. went on to say that our if-onlys fall into three categories: 1) matters that aren't serious enough to have a permanently damaging effect, when for example, a girl might say, "I could kick myself for telling Rex I already had a date with someone else; 2) matters that have some effect on the future but nothing serious enough to interfere with a normal life, for example, "I wish I had taken that after-school job even though it wasn't something I was dying to do; and 3) matters that result in disaster or tragedy, for example, "If only I had talked my sister out of riding with a guy who had been drinking."

I don't honestly know much about what went on for the rest of the period. All I could think about was John. I do remember we talked about some tragic things that happened in our community during the past year and whether or not they could have been prevented.

I had my tape recorder on, so later Miss Hambrick and I sorted the conversation out for the book. We didn't try to keep track of who said what. Just some of the incidents and whether or not they might have been preventable.

Most of us in Mr. Rickman's class thought especially of things that happened in our schools. We live in a college town that isn't big like a city but small enough that a major disaster affects the whole community. Naturally, the schools are rivals until something tragic happens. Like when John got killed in that accident, even kids who didn't know him felt bad. At a time like that, you find yourself thinking, It could have been me.

Some of the happenings the class mentioned were:

Three teenagers who drove into the side of a freight train on their way home from a kegger. The two boys killed, the girl so disfigured that even years of plastic surgery won't patch her up entirely. (Preventable. The kids were disobeying the law by drinking. Also, an adult furnished the liquor to the minors.)

A three-year-old boy beaten to death by his mother's live-in. (Preventable? Definitely!)

The tornado that destroyed part of our town. (Not preventable. A freak of nature. Probably not something we citizens should have prepared for because this area never had a tornado before.)

The measles epidemic that hit the college campus. One person died and a lot of students missed classes. (Might have been prevented; our class couldn't decide. There's a vaccine for measles now, but there may not have been when those guys were little kids getting their shots.)

One thing that really shook us was finding out that one of our high-school kids contracted the virus that causes AIDS. Sure, we learn all about the disease, what causes it, how to avoid it, all that kind of stuff. But when it happens to someone practically your own age—someone you know—it really gets your attention! Scary! And sad, sad, sad. Could it have been prevented? In this case yes. The boy's name isn't Carl, but I'll call him that. Carl did quite a bit of bragging about how many girls he made out with. That multisex bit we talk about in several of our classes. Now the question is, How many of Carl's partners are walking a tightrope, wondering...? Carl insists he always used condoms, but did he really? Or did he use them the right way—whatever that is? Or was this one of those cases where condoms don't work? No wonder our parents are scared.

Some Things We'd Like to Erase

Mr. Rickman suggested we dig up a scene from the past that we wish we could erase or handle differently. Think it through and decide whether or not we could have caused matters to go in a different direction than they did. Regardless of what might have been, we must now accept the reality that we can't do anything about that particular situation, but we may learn something from it that could help us with future decisions.

My own private question was one that hurt too much to talk about in class, but I wrote it for the book. Could John's death have been prevented? Maybe if he hadn't always been teaming up with guys who were doing reckless things. It was almost as if he was asking to get hurt.

Most of all, I keep asking myself, Could I have got John to take better care of himself? To quit drinking, for instance? I think the answer is no because I didn't own John. He wasn't about to let me make decisions for him. That's why he stayed the way he was and I stayed the way I am instead of our becoming like each other.

So what's the lesson I might learn from this? You have to keep on loving some people even when you don't approve of them. You can try to have an effect on the person's behavior, but even if you can't, you have to hang on to your own principles and not be dragged down by someone else.

27

Love, Danny

I couldn't wait to get to school on Tuesday of this week. That probably sounds unreal coming from a nonstudent kind of kid. As soon as the bell rang, I spoke before anyone else had a chance to. "I got a letter from Danfra."

"Danfra?" Rusty repeated the name as if he'd never heard it before. He probably hadn't, since he's out of touch with what's going on in class most of the time.

"Oh yes, *her*—" somebody began.

I interrupted right away because I knew by the emphasis on that word *her* that the rest of the sentence was going to be a put-down. (That's how good I've got at "reading" voices.) "She was in this class for a while," I began, then couldn't think what else to say about her.

Indy came to the rescue. "She's the gal who came the same day I did. I've been wondering what happened to her. What does her letter say, Kirk?"

I looked at Mr. Rickman. "Is it okay if I read it?" I asked.

"Sure. I've been wondering about her too."

My voice kept shaking while I read the letter, but no one made fun of me, and the class listened as if they were interested.

Dear Kirk:

I'm sorry I left so suddenly without telling you good-bye. I really did appreciate your being friends with me and Aaron. I kept remembering something you said. You said kids do grow up. I decided that doesn't just mean they finally get to be thirty or forty but that they can be different as grown-ups than they were as kids. That also went along with something Mr. Rickman said: that you can't change the world but you can do something about yourself.

94

We all looked at Mr. Rickman at that point. Rusty said, "Well, all right!"
Mr. R. looked the way a man might look if he's about to cry. I figured
he was feeling self-conscious, so I hurried on with reading the letter:

Anyway, I have some good news about my family. Someone
my mother met at the shelter where you went with me brought us to
this town. Of course, we got lined up with Social Services right
away and started through the same old red tape about food and
shelter and all that jazz. All of a sudden I got this brave streak and
decided to do something about myself. I said to the woman that I
wanted to learn how to make my own way so we wouldn't be on
welfare for the rest of our lives. My mom practically went into
shock. "Danfra!" she said. But the woman looked at me very
seriously. Finally she said: "That happens to be our theme song
here. We want people who don't have permanent homes to learn
how to manage their own lives. In fact, we have a project in this
town for people just like you."

My mother was leaning forward by this time with a hopeful
look on her face. Even Aaron was paying attention, and his mouth
was open the littlest bit instead of in that straight line the way he
usually looks. The very next day we were in a house. A filthy, bat-
tered one, but there was this really neat guy asking if we'd be willing
to work on the house to clean and fix it up if some people helped
us. You can bet we said yes. So ever since we've been painting and
scrubbing and mending screens and killing bugs and learning how
to fix electric appliances and stuff like that.

But, Kirk, here's the most important part. A group of young
college students have this project where they take kids like Aaron
and me around and teach us how to take pictures. They lend us
their cameras and show us how to use them. Aaron nearly went
crazy running around snapping everything in sight. One of the guys
said Aaron has great talent for picking out good subjects for
pictures. Like a dog watching over a litter of kittens, for instance,
and a shabby old man feeding a squirrel, and ghetto kids playing
ball with a stick for a bat. One of the college kids told Aaron he
might want to be a photographer for a living when he grows up.
You should have seen Aaron's face when he said that.

There's something else that's neat for me. On Saturdays I go to
a Santa Claus workshop where I get to help make toys and fix over
secondhand ones for parents who have hardly any money to buy
things for their kids for Christmas. That's great because poor

children will be getting something that isn't charity. Aaron and I know what it feels like to always be accepting things you can't pay for. One reason for the workshop is that it teaches people who are on welfare how to help others at the same time they are being helped.

I think I would like to be a social worker or a counselor or a teacher or someone like that who works with people. I forgot to tell you: Aaron and I are in school. It's like a dream to be going to the same school every day and to know we won't be jerked out. You must be wondering why this letter is written with good English and spelling and punctuation. It's because I went to my teacher the way you do to get help from Mrs. Atkins and asked her if she would help me to write this letter correctly. She actually hugged me. "You've made my day," she said. "Imagine a student *asking* for that kind of help!" Anyway, Kirk, I wanted you and Mr. Rickman to know that Aaron and I are on our way to growing up in more ways than just getting older.

Love, Danny

Whenever I read that part of the letter about Aaron, I feel as if I'm in his skin again, only now it feels great.

The room was dead quiet while I was reading the letter, but the kids started talking as soon as I finished, saying things like, "Hey, neat!" "Why don't we write to Danny?" "How come she signed it *Danny* instead of *Danfra*?" "Did you really go visit her at the shelter, Kirk?"

It was Vashti, the quiet, shy African-American girl who said: "I have an idea. Why couldn't we do something for Danny's family as our community-service project?"

The community-service project is part of the Reachout program at our school. It's the activity most students like best of anything we do all year. It's something we do as a service to the town. Things like getting acquainted with people at a retirement center and going to visit them and send them valentines; putting on entertainment for the kids at Children's Hospital; painting and repairing homes for people who are too poor or not well enough to take care of their own property; volunteering to go on cancer drives.

Someone mentioned that Danny's family isn't in our community anymore.

Mr. Rickman said we might do something that would count as community involvement since it would be a follow-up on a family who has been here recently.

We racked our brains and came up with a lot of suggestions that wouldn't work. Then it was Rusty — of all people — who had an idea that caught on. A car wash to raise money to buy a really good camera for Danfra and Aaron. We love car washes because you can make all the noise you want and let off a lot of steam and squirt water on one another between car jobs.

Mr. R. said: "I like the idea. Since good cameras can cost a lot of money, you could have your car wash, and then choose one that you can afford."

So that's our community-service project for this year, and we can hardly wait to get going on it.

By the way, my parents are enthusiastic about it too. I think Mom is secretly pleased that I'm corresponding with a girl my own age, and she and Dad are certainly pleased that I'm thinking about someone else's problems for a change.

Something to Consider

As a class you might want to "adopt" a family in your community. This might be a homeless family, the family of a newcomer to your school, a single-parent family, or another family with special needs. A committee from your class might approach the family by explaining that you want to help them to feel welcome and to enjoy being members of your town.

With the family's approval, activities could include:

1. Acting as big brothers or big sisters to children in the family and doing things with them during some out-of-school hours when parents are working.

2. Visiting with members who are sick or disabled. (Being careful, of course, not to be around anyone who might have a contagious illness.)

3. Sending family members greeting cards for special occasions.

4. Reading to children or visually handicapped members.

5. Shoveling walks, tending lawns, runnings errands on occasion if family members aren't able to do those things for themselves.

6. Tutoring children who are behind in school.

7. Most important of all, encouraging members of all ages to be as independent as possible.

28

Needed: One Adult

Mr. Rickman began one class by saying we were going to talk about transactional analysis. That turned me off right away, but then he drew circles on the board and gave some examples of what he was talking about, so I decided it was something I could handle after all.

"Everyone is made up of three beings," Mr. R. explained. "Child, parent, adult. Sometimes a person plays one role, sometimes another. When two or more people get together, they usually start communicating, either through words or actions. As long as their communication is appropriate—in other words, *fitting*—things probably go along smoothly. For instance, the parent tells her five-year-old to pick up his toys because it's bedtime.

"That's okay, because each individual is playing the intended role. Of course, the boy may argue or fool around or do some other five-year-old kind of thing until he discovers Mom means business. That's still all right because the kid is acting like a child, which is what he is, and the mother is acting like a parent. Are you with me so far?"

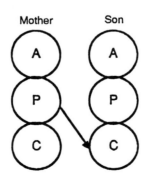

We told him yes, so he went on with the explanation: "The late psychiatrist Eric Berne, who came up with this idea of parent-adult-child, labeled the top circle *parent* and the middle one *adult*. I prefer to think of the top one as the adult part of the model, because I think of the adult role as the one often needed to keep a situation from falling apart. Let's call it the Rickman adaptation of p-a-c. You will see why Berne put it the other way around if you go into a study of transactional analysis, but for our purposes, my model will do. Okay?"

We readily agreed, not being wild to go into the study of anything.

"So all right, let's take another example. Now suppose this daughter is seventeen and her dad tells her she hasn't been getting enough sleep lately and had better be in bed by nine tonight. The father is placing the girl in the position of child, and the daughter isn't about to stand still for that. 'What do you think I am?' she asks. 'A child?'

"From there, communication goes downhill, because the daughter considers herself adult enough to be capable of deciding what time to be in bed."

"What's an example of a kid playing the role of parent?" Marcie asked.

Mr. R. said: "Suppose a twelve-year-old girl comes home from school and finds her mother crying. She probably reacts just as a parent does when the child cries, which is to ask, 'What's the matter?'

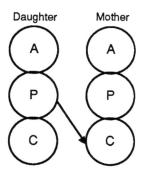

"The mother may react in one of three ways. As a parent: 'It's nothing, Dear. Don't you be worrying about things that don't concern you.' As a child 'Don't bother me. Just leave me alone!' As an adult: 'I'm upset about a family matter, and I'd like to talk it over with you, because it concerns you too'."

Mr. R. said, "Notice that with this last approach, the mother places herself and the daughter in new roles:

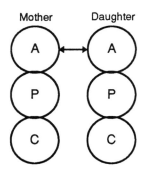

"The mother goes on to say: 'Your father and I are not getting along, and we feel the family may be better off if we get a divorce. How do you feel about it, Jane?'

"Now Jane may react in one of the three ways. As a child: 'I want my daddy. Don't send him away.' As a parent: 'I think you and Dad should try harder to get along.' As an adult: 'Who will make a living for us if Daddy and you get a divorce? Where will I live?'"

When Mr. Rickman asked us to give examples from our own lives, we really got carried away:

Matt: When my dad was driving me to the dentist yesterday, some nutty guy walked right in front of us on the red light. Dad stuck his head out of the window and yelled, "Hey, you trying to get killed or something?" I guess he was being a parent to the man.

Nanette: My mom was sick when I got home from school one day. I told her to go to bed, and I'd get supper. That's being a parent to your mom.

Rusty: My dad got drunk last night and poured a cup of coffee all over the table. How's that for being a child?

Mr. R. said those were excellent examples. So what can we do with this kind of knowledge to make it work for us?

"Try to act like adults, I suppose," some bright kid suggested.

Mr. R. nodded. "Many situations need at least one adult. In cases where there's a bad scene, it's often because all the people involved react like children. Or maybe someone is being the heavy parent. Suppose your father says you can't be in sports anymore until you bring your grades up. What might your reactions be?"

We had a lot of answers for that: Argue. Get mad. Leave home. Sneak out of the house. Get worse grades. Go to your room and sulk.

Mr. R. said, "So far no one has suggested the reaction that would solve the problem."

"You mean get better grades?"

"Why not?"

"Then your dad would figure he had you under his thumb."

"Why not?"

"Well, you can't let him think he has that much control over you."

"Even if it solves the problem?" Mr. R. asked. "What you are saying isn't consistent. You are saying a childish reaction is preferable to the most adult of the responses, which would be to improve your grades. You would rather do something to prove you are a child, so your parents can feel justified in treating you like one."

"Well, if we keep doing everything they say, *that* proves we're children," Evan argued.

"Not if what you do is mature behavior. If you want to get your parents off your backs, start being good parents to yourselves. But if you prove you need them, they'll be right there breathing on you."

Wow! Maybe Rickman really has something. What if I took on the adult role and cleaned the garage tomorrow before my dad tells me to? Maybe I'll just give it a try. Depends on how grown-up I feel tomorrow.

Something to Observe

Our assignment was to observe pairs or groups of people to see what roles—child, parent, or adult—they were playing. Tell how you would rate each example: Successful communication? Bad-news relationship?

It was Indy's suggestion that the class role-play some of the situations. Class members could suggest how someone's playing a different role (child, parent, or adult) might have produced a different result.

Mr. Rickman instructed the class to watch for scenes of mob violence or other out-of-control group behavior either on TV or through firsthand observation. What roles were the participants playing? If police were involved, what role were they playing? If someone managed to get control of the crowd or part of it in order to reason with the troublemakers, what role was that person playing? Was the overall outcome costly in terms of money, property damage, human injury, or human life?

29

Who Needs Parenting?

We students do a lot of griping about school. It's boring. We don't learn anything. It's like being in prison. The stuff we learn isn't relevant.

Actually, it's not all that bad though. Like in Human Behavior, we had this big discussion about discipline. Mr. Rickman said that's certainly relevant because everyone is subject to discipline all the time. Besides, someday many of us will be parents, and discipline will be one of our major worries. He told us he wasn't going to give a lecture. Instead, he wanted our ideas. Kids have good ideas, he said. So what choice did we have after that remark but to come up with some? (Teachers are tricky.)

As it turned out, we did a good job with the discussion. Some of the conclusions we arrived at made us sound like experts on the subject of discipline.

We started out arguing about different ways of making kids mind and about whether it's better to be bossy or easygoing and what to do if your kid refuses to eat and stuff like that. We decided there's no exactly right way to handle a specific problem. After all, we kids in that class were brought up by different methods, and we turned out okay. (Our parents may not think so, but we agreed we're all right most of the time.)

So we concluded if it wasn't entirely the methods our parents used on us, it must be the way they felt about us. Finally we summed it up (with a little help from the teacher) like this:

1. the parent must feel good about the child,

2. the child must feel good about the parent,

3. the parent must feel good about himself or herself,

4. the child must feel good about herself or himself.

We decided to call this "okayness."

If the child and the parent feel all right about each other most of the time, then the parent will be sensible in the matter of discipline, and the child will be able to take the punishment because of knowing the parent cares about him or her. The punishment will seem more fair if the feelings between child and parent are warm and caring.

Another thing we agreed on was that it's pretty important what kind of person the parent is. The parent has to like himself or herself and have self-confidence. Also, the parent should be the kind of person the kids can like and admire. There's not much point in parents telling kids what they ought to do if the kids don't like the way their parents are. We especially mentioned that parents should have a sense of humor. So should teachers. (At this point Mr. Rickman said, "Aren't you the lucky ones to have me for your teacher?")

Our cue was to laugh, and we did.

Mr. R. put in some of his ideas too. Every child needs parenting. He said that doesn't mean every child has to have two good parents in order to grow up sound (it would help though). However, every child needs some adult guidance to set up standards.

Nedra said this amounts to imposing adult values on the kid.

Mr. R. pointed out that a child must learn from the adult world what is acceptable and what's not. We aren't born knowing that, and we don't pick it up without someone helping us to realize what works and what doesn't.

That makes good sense, but then we got into a discussion about how setting standards might discourage children from doing their own thinking.

Mr. R. didn't think this would be a problem if the child has a chance to help set the standards. Like helping to make household rules and deciding what happens if they are broken. He said, as preteens and teens, we should be setting many of our own guidelines and managing ourselves well enough that adults can feel comfortable about not interfering too much.

Lance had some comment about teens not having enough freedom. That gave Mr. R. a chance to work one of his favorite quotations into the conversation. It was from the poet Robert Frost, who said freedom is "when you're easy in your harness."

We spent some time complaining about how parents treat us like little kids.

Mr. R. said, "That's because you keep them anxious and scared. You break out of harness."

One of the really important points Mr. R. made was that parenting should be a temporary condition. He explained it sort of like this: "Let's assume that a doctor-patient relationship is a kind of parenting—doctor telling patient what to do for his or her own good. The same is true in other helping combinations such as psychiatrist-patient, teacher-pupil, counselor-client, Scout leader-child, parent-child, relative or foster parent-child, lawyer-client. These temporary relationships are designed to guide a person (or group) to a healthier, more stable, more independent state.

It's all a matter of growing up, and growing up means *growing away from*. If parents have to keep on telling sons and daughters what to do when they are practically grown, there's something wrong."

Mr. Rickman reminded us it can be even more difficult for parents to outgrow parenthood than for children to outgrow childhood.

I'm going to mention that to my parents. Better wait a few days, though, till they quit smarting over my staying at a party until one in the morning without phoning them.

Some Individual Activities to Choose From

Each student in Mr. R.'s class was given a choice of one of the following two activities:

1. Do a bulletin board on parenting. Show examples such as doctor-patient, teacher-pupil, family scenes. Include the lighter side of playing the role of parent through jokes, cartoons, and amusing newspaper and magazine write-ups.

2. Bring to class examples from home, school, or elsewhere of people acting in the role of parent to others.

Something to Work on As a Class Project

Your class might research and prepare a panel discussion on the major types of discipline:

1. authoritarian (bossy: <u>Do as I say</u>),

2. permissive (kid directed: <u>Have your own way, dear</u>),

3. laissez-faire, pronounced "les-ay-fair" (little or no direction: <u>You're on your own</u>).

Mr. R. defined *laissez-faire* as a French term meaning noninterference, freedom of action, letting matters take their own course. As a discipline method, it means giving kids little or no help with decision making—leaving too much up to them.

30

I Believe...

My parents and I got into a hassle about what we believe in. It started when the subject of our neighbors, Althea Carter and Ron Beard, came up. Althea is white, Ron is black, and they're living together.

My mom said it's bad enough when people of different races marry, but it's even worse when they live together out of wedlock.

I asked why it's worse, and that really set things in motion. I got the lecture about the present generation and its lack of morals.

I said the problem is that older people won't accept change, and there has to be change or society will atrophy. (Mr. Rickman told us that, and I thought it sounded pretty impressive, but it didn't go over so well with my parents.) Dad said society had just as well atrophy as go downhill. Then I started talking about what a concerned generation we are: worried about the mess the world is in, wanting to bring an end to wars....

I shouldn't have mentioned war, because Dad launched into the speech about how we're a generation of cop-outs, pretending to hate war just because we haven't the guts to fight for our country.

Mom interrupted at that point. "That's not fair, Ray. I think it's commendable that our young people deplore war."

"I suppose you think it's commendable when they burn draft cards and go slinking off to Canada."

"Well no," she admitted, "but I do hope Kirk is one of today's young people who don't glorify war." She didn't ask me whether I am or not. Just talked about me as if I wasn't there.

"There does come a time when you have to defend your country," my father reminded her.

"Well, yes, but.... Mom saw she was getting snowed on that argument, so she switched the scene back to me. "What bothers me, Kirk, is that lately you disagree with everything your dad and I believe in. It just isn't like you."

"That's because I'm not a little kid anymore. Children believe what their parents tell them, but when they get to be teenagers, they start doing their own thinking."

"Sounds like some of the propaganda they feed you at school," my dad put in.

"Well, you *do* want me to do my own thinking, don't you?"

"That depends on what you think," Dad answered.

"See, that's the whole point. As long as I think like you, it's great, but when I start thinking like me...!"

"Kirk, stop shouting," my mother said, looking nervous.

I thought about something I had read in a book about kids and parents. It said that when grown-ups start closing in on you, it's because they're scared. I wondered if my parents were scared about something.

"Look," I said, "I haven't done anything very terrible, have I? Sure, my grades aren't so hot, but I'm working on that. I haven't been in trouble with the law. I'm not hung up on drugs. Actually I'm quite a kid."

We all laughed then, and that relieved the tension.

"We know you are, Kirk," Mom said, "and we want to keep it that way."

"I won't always do just what you think I should," I warned them. "But you've done a good job with me, so I ought to wind up okay."

"Of course you will," Dad said. His tone said I'd *better*.

"It's just that you don't seem to believe the way we do anymore," Mom said again. "It's like you reject all of our ideas."

I started to argue about that, but then I decided maybe she's right. Every time she or Dad brings something up, I get on the defensive.

"Maybe it's because you two get so worked up about things," I suggested. "Like the matter of Althea and Ron. So what?"

"So what!" Mom exclaimed.

"I think I see what Kirk means," Dad said. "How are we affected by what Ron and Althea do?"

I put into words what my mom was probably thinking: "You're afraid it will happen to us."

"I suppose that's about it," Dad admitted. "You see all the deplorable things going on around you, and you wonder if you'll be next."

I said, "That's what Mr. Dean would call 'worrying ahead of time.'"

"I suppose," Mom said. "Well, Kirk, we do appreciate you, even if you don't see things our way."

"Well, whatever I am, it's all you guys' fault. Those pesky little genes I was born with, and all these years of discipline."

So after all, it turned out to be a pretty good session. It wound up with all of us laughing and feeling more relaxed with one another but still believing the way we did in the first place.

Something to Argue About

As usual our homework this week is something having to do with people, including ourselves. Mr. Rickman says learning how to do a better job of living is like any other skill. Take tennis, for instance. You get a lot of information about rackets, balls, courts, and so forth. Then you learn the rules of the game and how it's played. After that, you play it, and you keep practicing until it comes easier. Mr. R. says anything is difficult until it becomes easy. So learning about coping with problems and dealing with people isn't complete until we've tried out what we know in our everyday lives to find out what works and what doesn't.

Since we have been talking about prejudice in Human Behavior, I told the class about the Althea-Ron discussion with my parents. Mr. R. said this would be a good time to examine some of our beliefs about life and people. He instructed us to list some of our own beliefs and some of our parents' beliefs that are cause for argument or debate. I think Mr. R. has in mind for us to do something more with those lists later on. Meantime, we are to report in class about conflicts with parents, teachers, or someone else over something we disagreed about. We are supposed to keep in mind that these arguments aren't a matter of who's right and who's wrong but of people seeing the same thing in different ways.

31

I Believe, You Believe, We Believe...

Sure enough, the I-believe, you-believe lesson wasn't finished. The next day Mr. R. started off by saying that young people and parents are in conflict because they think they are farther apart than they really are. He drew a circle on the board and labeled it "Parents' values."

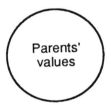

"As long as you are children," he said, "your beliefs are practically the same as your parents' with some influence from certain other adults in your life: teachers, relatives, youth leaders, for instance. That's how a value system is built; it is handed down from a preceding generation."

He drew another circle approximately on top of the first one to show how parents' and children's values overlap.

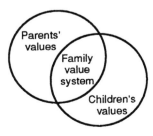

"So far not much conflict," he pointed out. "Of course, there will be minor differences in belief. For example, the parent may think eight is an appropriate bedtime for the six-year-old, while the child might cherish the belief that kids should go to bed whenever they darn please.

"Differences aren't so minor, though, when this child becomes a preteen. By now he or she has been exposed to many beliefs besides those of parents: values picked up from friends, movies, books, TV, society in general. The result is a state of confusion. Parents, anxious over the conflict, try to reinforce their own standards. The young person experiences anxiety, too, afraid of being only a shadow of adults, especially parents. In order to establish his or her own identity, the kid begins struggling out of those smothering adult values. The result is a tendency to reject *all* the indoctrination of the growing-up years to this point."

"That's what my parents said," I interrupted. "They claim I argue with everything they say, and as a matter of fact, I just about do."

Mr. R. said, "Well, when I'm through with this fascinating lecture, you won't have to anymore, because you'll understand how come you're going through this obnoxious stage." He drew two more circles to represent the teenager's and parents' values.

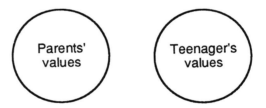

"You'll notice this circle is separate from the other. The young person is determined it must be completely different from the parent circle. Now why doesn't that work?"

Because you're bound to believe some of the same things your parents do, we decided.

"Exactly. Let's move the circle." Mr. R. made a new drawing to show the overlapping of parent-teen beliefs.

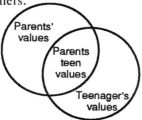

"Why do you have some of your parents' ideas?" he asked.

Because some of them are good, we told him.

"Right," Mr. R. agreed. "Besides it isn't easy to shrug off something that has been built into a person for years. It's like the weaving of a tapestry. There's one integrated design that is you. You might pull out a few threads, but if you pull all of them, the thing falls apart. Now how can you build your own value system and at the same time reassure your parents?"

"By letting them know a lot of your beliefs are the same as theirs," I said.

"Yes. And the ones that are the same are usually the solid, important ones. For instance, your generation and my generation may hold different beliefs about the sanctity of marriage, but both of us probably believe that a child needs to be cared for by concerned adults. You may not have the same religious beliefs as your parents, but probably you and they recognize that there is some power greater than we are to have created the universe."

Our written assignment was to make three lists: Things I believe in that my parents (or surrogate parents) don't. Things my parents believe in that I don't. Things my parents and I both believe.

"You may find that third list to be the longest after all," Mr. R. said.

We talked about how to decide what values to choose. Mr. R. said part of our confusion is due to having so many systems to select from. What we were brought up to believe may be in conflict with what modern society adopts.

"We shouldn't believe something just because someone tells us we should," Matt said.

We said he was right about that, but then, how *do* we decide? We finally came to the conclusion that our philosophies have to be what makes sense to us.

Mr. R. said that's a good criterion. He said if we examine the values we were brought up with, we'll find that many of them make sense. Then we can afford to agree with our parents at least some of the time. That way they won't be so upset when we disagree.

Something to Share with Parents

Mr. R. had in mind for us to do something with those lists. We were to divide a sheet of paper in thirds lengthwise. The left third was to be labeled My Values. The right third was Parents' Values or only one parent's values if preferred. The middle third was for beliefs that are held by both kid and parents. These may be values that are similar but differ somewhat. For instance, my folks and I believe family members should all know where the others are when they're apart, but I don't think I should be expected to phone home every time I go from one place to another all evening. That's what my mom thinks I should do. After all, I'm not ten years old! Sophie had the best paper, so we chose it for the book:

My Values (Sophie) What I Believe	Our Values: Mine and Mom's What Mom & I Both Believe	Parent's Values (Sophie's Mom) What My Mother Believes
1. being honest	1. being honest	1. being honest
2. concern for others	2. concern for others	2. concern for others
3. some abortions okay	13. listen to all sides of question	3. all abortions a sin
4. less work, more fun	15. accept consequences of own behavior	4. more work, less fun
5. obey laws that make sense		5. obey all laws
6. okay to waste time		6. make every minute count
7. share troubles with others	*beliefs of my mom and me that are similar, but somewhat modified*	7. keep troubles to yourself
8. protest marches and demonstrations okay	firm discipline of children, but punishment must not be bigger than the misbehavior	8. demonstrations a waste of time
9. discipline kids, but not too strictly		9. firm discipline, stiff punishment
10. some divorces justified	Mom may be right about obeying all laws, because some would make sense to some people and not to others	10. divorce is a sin
11. occasional use of alcohol		11. no alcohol, ever!
12. abolish capital punishment		12. believe in capital punishment
13. listen to all sides of question	More work, less fun: I think Mom should work less, and she thinks I should work more. Maybe both right	13. listen to all sides of question
14. give children lots of freedom		14. be protective of children at all times
15. accept consequences of own behavior	freedom for children: Mom is *overly*protective, but many parents aren't enough	15. accept consequences of own behavior
16. belief in greater power, not necessarily God		16. belief in God and church attendance
17. don't worry about what others think of you	sharing troubles: I don't think people should be talking about their problems to just anyone, but do some sharing	17. it matters what others think about you
18. Gays different sexually, not weird or deranged		18. Gays unnatural and sinful
19. education and training, not necessarily college		19. college for everyone

32

Sticks and Stones

In counseling group the subject of prejudice came up. It started with Sally complaining because her folks object to her dating a Korean boy.

"That's one trouble with the older generation," Morris said. "They're prejudiced."

"Are you?" Mr. Dean asked.

We told him we aren't. Oh, maybe some of our generation, but not us in the group.

"Let me try out some designations on you and see if you object to them. How about *nigger*?"

We objected to that one and also to *wop, spick, chink, kike, imbecile, moron, idiot, faggot, fag.*

We couldn't agree about *Mexican*. It depends on how it's used and who is using it, but in general we said we prefer *Hispano* or *Hispanic*.

"In other words, it's the connotation of the word, rather than the word itself, that is significant."

We agreed.

"But in general," Mr. Dean said, "you object to words that demean, that cut down a person or a group."

Again we agreed, but I had a hunch we were about to walk into a trap.

Sure enough. "How do you feel about the word *pig*?" Mr. Dean asked.

By this time I knew this was something Miss Hambrick and Mr. Rickman would want in the book, so I got permission from Mr. Dean and the group to tape the rest of the conversation as long as I didn't use our real names. The discussion went like this:

Bill: If you're talking about animals....

Mr. Dean: I'm not talking about animals.

Bill: Well, if you mean cops, that's different from those other things you asked us.

Mr. D.: How different?

Allison: Well, like those other terms are minority groups.

Mr. D.: So are police officers.

Me: Can't you imagine how our friends would react if we referred to them as "police officers"?

Mr. D.: Yesterday evening a neighbor — a high-school kid — told me someone had stolen his motorcycle. When I asked him what he did about it, he said he called the police. Does your age group perhaps think of them as *police* when you need them and *pigs* when you don't?

Jean: I don't see what that has to do with prejudice.

Mr. D.: Perhaps your generation's view of the police is a form of prejudice.

Rob: Prejudice has to do with race and religion.

Mr. D.: *Prejudice* simply means a judgment that is built on emotion rather than reason or logic.

Morris: Getting back to the subject of the police. Adults believe in obeying a law whether it's good or not. Personally, I believe in obeying laws that make sense to me.

Mr. D.: Suppose everyone did that. Child beating makes sense to some people. So do things like fraud and censorship.

Sally: Well, *that* kind of thing....

Mr. D.: Who decides *what* kind of thing is all right? One of my counselees argues that vandalism and theft are okay because material things aren't important, so it doesn't matter what happens to them.

Rob: That's stupid.

Mr. D.: Not to that particular girl. Legalization of narcotics seems stupid to me, but it doesn't to the lawmakers in England.

Morris: Then you're saying we should obey laws whether they're dumb or not?

Mr. D.: That's exactly what I'm saying. We can go through certain channels to change laws and rules, but existing ones should be obeyed.

We groaned about that and argued some more. Then we got back to talking about prejudice. Mr. Dean said, "This subject reminds me of the childhood chant, 'Sticks and stones can break my bones, but what you say can't hurt me.' Of course, that isn't true; name-calling and other verbal insults are the sticks and stones that bruise on the inside, where it doesn't show."

For once, we didn't have any wise-off answers. Maybe we were all remembering some of those spoken sticks and stones from our own lives.

Mr. Dean said most of us probably have some prejudices, due to what we have been taught or to certain experiences we have had.

"One freedom no one can rob us of is the right to our own beliefs," Mr. Dean reminded us. He said it's not so important what our prejudice is as what we do about it. If someone is made to suffer because of our beliefs, we are going beyond the right to think whatever we want to.

We also talked about prejudice in Human Behavior class.

Margarita Flores was born in Mexico but has spent most of her life here. She likes being in this country but is proud of being Mexican. She thinks Mexico's music and dances and clothes are more exciting than ours. She also prefers Mexican food. Margarita is popular with the kids at school. Mr. R. says that's probably because she feels good about herself.

The African-American kids in the class are Daren and Vashti. Daren's just another kid, a regular guy, so we don't think about him as being different.

He said, "You guys might not think of me as a black, but you can sure bet I do."

Mr. R. asked him why.

His answer was something like this: "Suppose you were one of only a few whites in a black school. You would be different, and you would *feel* different. All the time."

"But you fit in so well," Sophie told him.

He said, "That's on account of people who treat me okay. But it doesn't make me feel like a white person. People aren't really 'color-blind' when it comes to skin color, so we shouldn't pretend to be."

Mr. R. asked Vashti how she feels about being black. I didn't expect her to answer. Vashti practically never says anything—just sort of melts into her classes. She's not rejected, but it's easy to ignore her. It was surprising that she bothered to answer, but the real surprise was what she said. "It's not being black that makes me feel different; it's that my dad is in prison."

We all sat there not knowing what to say. It was like in those fairy tales where a spell is cast over everyone. While we were wondering what to do, Indy went over to Vashti and put her arms around her. Since I'm not a little kid anymore, I don't cry (except when John died), but now my throat felt choky and there was a prickly feeling like splinters behind my eyes.

After a minute or so, Indy hugged Vashti and went back to her own desk.

Mr. R. said just the right thing: "Remember, Vashti, it isn't *you* who are in prison; it's your father."

Something to Ask Yourself

Our assignment was to prepare to discuss what our prejudices are, if any, and to identify the reason for each one. Do we consider our so-called prejudices reasonable or unreasonable? Do any of them affect our behavior toward other people? In other words, do we simply feel prejudice, or is our treatment of some people affected by our feeling about them? In what way is prejudice different from dislike? Is there a difference between prejudice and discrimination? We had to be ready to give examples.

33

Things I Wish People Would Say to Me

We should know better than to complain in English class, because Mrs. Atkins turns our grousing into assignments. For instance, the other day Marcie mentioned that she was tired of being criticized all the time. We fell into that trap right away with a bunch of remarks like: "Every morning it's the same old thing: Why don't you make your bed?" "Why do you have to look as if you'd slept in your clothes?" "When are you going to get that hair cut?" "Why can't you get good grades like your sister?" Then we come to school, and it starts all over again: "Where's the assignment that was due last week?" "Why can't you get to class on time?" "Where were you yesterday when we talked about adverbs and adjectives?" "How come you blew that test?" "When are you going to shape up in this class?"

"Why don't you knock it off?" Mrs. Atkins interrupted at that point. "Now the title for today's assignment is Things I Wish People Would Say to Me."

We looked shocked and said, "Huh?" and a few other dumb things.

Mrs. Atkins said: "The assignment is just what it says. So pick up your pencils and start writing."

I did, and the assignment just poured itself out onto paper in a natural sort of way.

I wish my mom would say: "Kirk, I like the way your're wearing your hair these days. Those patches on your jeans are great. Where did you get the idea of making them all different colors? You made your bed a couple of times this week. That's really something! You know, Kirk, I'm glad we have you instead of that mama's boy next door. I've been thinking about what you said about not wanting to go on vacation with Dad and me next summer. A boy your age is old enough to make up his own mind about things like that. One thing I really enjoy is your sense of humor. Come to think about it, you're a fun person to have around."

I wish my dad would say: "Kirk, it's great that you want to do your own thinking. You have some really sensible ideas. Like why shouldn't teenagers be allowed to take whatever they want to in school? Your mother and I are proud of you for staying in school when so many kids are dropping out. It really isn't important that you aren't on the honor roll. What counts is that you're just a regular guy. We really like you just the way you are."

I wish my teachers would say: "That was a good paper you wrote, even if it was late and you spelled forty words wrong. I was pleased with you for asking a question in class yesterday just when you kids were getting bored. You'll never be a great student, but you do think about things. That's better than memorizing a bunch of junk for a good grade on a test. I'm proud of you for being at school most of the time. You don't use sickness as a cop-out the way so many kids do."

Shannon and I don't see each other much anymore. I think she's outgrowing me. It doesn't bother me as much as I thought it would. I was always wishing she would say something like: "I know you have to have a life of your own. It's okay with me if you do things with other people. I love you because you're so strong, and you make me feel safe. I know you're smart, too, even if your grades don't show it. I can tell by the way you figure things out about people. You really do seem to understand people. That's a lot more important than knowing math and stuff like that."

That's all the time I had before the bell rang, but it pretty well summed up how I want people to see me. Mrs. Atkins wrote on the paper: "Great job! And on time!"

Something to Wish For

Mrs. Atkins's pupils liked the I-wish assignment. Her comment was: "I wish you were always as enthusiastic about writing as you were on this job."

Members of your class might enjoy doing this assignment. Discuss the value of such an exercise: What might it tell about the writer's self-esteem? How might it give a different picture of a person from the one seen by the people close to him or her?

34

Things I Forgot to Tell You

Next day Mrs. Atkins talked about our papers on things we wish people would tell us. She said: "You know, people may be thinking some of those things, even if they don't say them. However, we do need to be built up from time to time so we'll know we're okay." She stopped talking long enough for that to sink in but not long enough for us to start acting up.

Then she said: "Often people forget to tell you the good things about yourselves. But maybe you do the same thing with them. You don't bother to say what *they* want to hear."

Oh, oh, I thought. Here it comes: the new assignment. And sure enough. Mrs. Atkins said: "Today put your pencils to work on this title: Things I Forgot to Tell You. Write as if you were talking to someone in your life who counts."

We groaned, of course. Mrs. Atkins said: "If you can talk, you can write. And heaven knows you can talk."

I decided to write my paper to my parents. Seemed like a good idea, seeing that we haven't been getting along too swift this week.

I was so built up because Mrs. Atkins had liked my other paper that I felt like really going to work on this one. She's right. It's something what a little praise can do.

My paper went like this:

Dear Mom and Dad,

There are some really great things I remember about you from my growing-up years. I should have mentioned them at the time, but you know how it is with a dumb kid.

Anyway, there was that time when I was a little guy working on my model cars. I got a smear of red paint on that gray desk. Mom, I could tell how upset you were when you saw it. After all, you had worked a long time finishing that desk. When you saw the paint, I figured you were going to land all over me. Believe me, I was scared. I said, "Don't you think red paint looks sort of nice on the furniture in a boy's room?" At first I thought you were going to yell at me, but then suddenly you laughed. "I guess it might be a good color for a boy's room at that," you said. I thought at the time how lucky I was to have a mother who could laugh about something like that. Wish I'd thought to mention it.

There was something else in those days. You drove me to school, Mom. It was too far to walk in bad weather, and the school bus didn't come near our house. I used to think I'd die if any of the guys saw me riding with my mother. That probably hurt your feelings. It didn't have anything to do with you though. It's just that boys in grade school don't want to be seen with their mothers. You didn't make a big deal of it though. In fact, you would let me off a block away from school. You even let me crouch down under the dashboard after you stopped the car. That way I could open the car door a crack and peek out. One time you even told me that Jason McDermott was passing by. So we waited for him to go on before I crept out of the car. It might be a little late, but thanks for understanding how it feels to be eight years old.

Dad, the latest thing you did that I want to thank you for was the night last month when I got hauled down to the police station for being at that party where some of the kids were smoking grass. I know anything to do with drugs seems like the end of the world to parents. I wasn't one of the kids smoking, but the trouble was, I was there. I can imagine how you must have felt when you got a call late at night saying your kid was in trouble. I thought you would half kill me. As it was, you weren't easy on me. That's about my worst night so far. But when you walked into the police station, you said: "That's my son. I'd like to take him home and work this out." I wouldn't have thought much about it except that Ross Mercer's dad took one look at Ross and yelled: "That's no son of mine! He got himself in here. Now we'll see how he gets himself out." I know I'm always griping because you and Mom treat me like a little kid. At the same time, though, it sure feels great to have parents who still claim you even when you disgrace them.

When I have kids of my own, I'll do some things different than you two do. But you have taught me right from wrong, even if I don't always stick to what's right. I gave you a bad time because you wouldn't write an excuse for me when I cut school that day a bunch of us eighth-graders took off on a sneak day like the one the high-school seniors take every year. A lot of parents made up false excuses for their kids. I felt sort of proud down deep, though, to know you wouldn't lie for me. Made me feel that since you don't lie *for* me, you probably don't lie *to* me either.

Well, it's about time for the bell, so I'll drag this to a close. Love ya both, even if I do act crappy a lot of the time.

Your son, Kirk

Mrs. Atkins actually told me I have a real gift for writing when I get wound up with what I'm saying. Imagine me with a gift that has anything to do with schoolwork!

"I hope you give this letter to your parents," Mrs. Atkins said. Well, I don't really think I'd have the nerve to do that. Boy, but two *A*s in one week! You know, I just *might* show that letter to my folks. Maybe....

Some Things to Remember

Because Mrs. Atkins's pupils scored well on their I-wish assignment, they worked especially hard on the I-forgot one. Most of them decided to rewrite their letters, correcting the errors, and to give them or send them to the people they were meant for.

Your class might want to discuss how this assignment can make us aware of how much easier it is to criticize than to compliment.

35

Hatefully Yours

"Today you're going to write a letter to your parents," Mrs. Atkins told us on Monday.

"Oh no!" Chip said. "We just got through seeing them. Like less than an hour ago."

"Quit whining and get out your pencils."

Quite a few of us didn't have pencils and paper, of course, so we got a five-minute lecture on being responsible. It's like everyone's expecting us to grow up all at once.

"Naturally you wouldn't expect to have to do any writing in an English class," Mrs. Atkins said, glaring at us.

"Nobody cares how we feel," Chip complained.

Mrs. Atkins said: "Well, you're just about to have a chance to tell somebody. That's exactly what these letters are all about."

"Couldn't we just *tell* you?" I asked. "Out loud, I mean."

"No, I want these to be written messages. However, these letters will not be sent or given to your parents unless you want them to be. But write them as if you were talking to your parents. Tell them how you feel about things. I'm tired of hearing you complain about nobody understanding you. Here is a chance to get a grade for complaining."

The next day Mrs. Atkins asked if we minded if she shared parts of our letters with the class as long as the writers' names weren't given. She had made copies of these, and she would like for us to read them to ourselves if it was okay with us. (We were probably thinking that would beat having to do a written assignment, so we told her we didn't mind a bit.)

She went on to say she had corrected our spelling and punctuation, so we could wade through the assignment without all the misery teachers have to go through in reading papers.

The parts of the letters she gave us to read were:

Dear Parents,

For once would you get out of your narrow world and hear what I'm saying? I'm thirteen years old and fed up with your not paying attention to what's going on in our lives. I know your jobs take up a great part of your time, but think about *me*. Is life just eating, sleeping, working, and watching TV?

Dear Grown-ups:

As I sit here trying to figure out just what I think of grown-ups, I can think of no words — only a great heap of emotions that are about to split me wide open at the seams. I suppose I have the same gripes as other kids. When are you going to let go of me?

Dear Mom,

Just wanted to say good-bye. I'll be cutting out soon. Taking a "little vacation." Just like the one Dad took five years ago. You know the one; he's still on it. I haven't known you, and you haven't known me since third grade. I know how awful you feel about Dad's leaving us, but remember, I feel awful too.

Dear Mother and Father:

If you tell me I can't do something, have a reason. Quit treating me like a little kid, and don't spend so much time worrying about what the neighbors will think.

Dear Mom,

There are a few things I should tell you that have been on my mind. Remember when I wanted that formal, and you said it cost too much? You shot me down, Mom. That formal was *really* important to me.

Dear Mom:

I don't know what's happened between us these past two years, but I just don't like you anymore. Everything you do gets on my nerves. I think one reason you don't like me is because my dad thinks a lot of me, and you want all his love. You also think you are an expert on everything. Why don't you realize your mistakes and faults before it's too late?

Dear Folks:

I get sick and tired of you telling me what to do and what not to do. It just so happens I am going to make my own choices, and you can't take that away from me!

The way it turned out, Mrs. Atkins did have a written assignment in mind for us after all. She said: "Pretend you are the parents of the writers of these letters. Pretend you actually received one of them. Write down what feelings you have."

After we had been writing for a little while, she had us read our lists while she wrote the emotions on the board: guilty, sad, ashamed, mad, hurt, disappointed, surprised, annoyed, uptight, furious.

"I don't see any satisfying emotions here," Mrs. Atkins commented. "All unhappy, I'd say."

"You told us to write what we were feeling and what we wanted our parents to know," we reminded her.

She said, "I guess we would have to end all these letters *Hatefully yours.*

"You didn't want us to write a bunch of stuff that isn't true just to make our parents feel good, did you?" Doug asked.

"Not really," she said. "There's nothing wrong with what you said. Many complaints of teenagers are fair: Parents not talking to you and not listening to you. Not treating your friends well. Grown-ups not understanding you. Not letting you grow up. Too much pressure. No, it's not what you said that bothers me."

"Must be the way we said it," someone suggested.

Mrs. Atkins nodded. "Exactly. What kind of reaction do we get from people when we cut them down? When we make them feel bad about themselves?"

"Not a very good reaction," Indy said.

"That's right," the teacher agreed. "The way we act grows out of how we feel. When people feel bad, they usually act that way. Now suppose you are the parent receiving a hatefully-yours letter. Are you going to change and start being a good parent all at once?"

Several of us gave opinions about that: "I'd feel so bad that I'd reform." "It would make me mad, so I'd treat the kid worse than ever." "I'd cry." "I'd decide I was a failure and give up." "I'd think my son or daughter was wrong and that I was a good parent." "I'd decide the kid was wrong and start building up my own case. We'd probably have a big fight."

Mrs. Atkins said: "Okay. So when you toss out criticism of the sort we just read, it's like giving someone a handful of barbed wire; it smarts. This kind of criticism amounts to an attack, though not all of your letters were like this. Tomorrow we'll look at some samples of suggestions that feel more like warm fur and less like thistles."

Mrs. Atkins's assignment was for the students to write down two or more gripes they would like to tell their parents if they had the nerve to do so. Then follow each complaint with what the student thinks the parents' response would be. For example: I'm tired of being treated like a child. Parents' response: Then quit acting like one.

36

And Lovingly Yours

Some teachers forget where they left off in class the day before, but not Mrs. Atkins. She plunges right in as if we've only been gone a minute.

The day after we wrote the complaining letters, she said: "You were wondering why we should write about our feelings. Writing is a message *from* someone *to* someone. The writer wants to convey how he or she feels or thinks. The purpose of the message may be to cause the person who receives it to believe or think as you do. Some of the letters we read yesterday would not do that. Some of the things we say to our parents don't do it either."

"Grown-ups won't listen to us," Ruth said in a complaining voice.

"That depends on the way you say it," Mrs. Atkins said. "Remember, when you hand someone a thistle, he or she is going to drop it."

She started passing papers around. "Try these on for size," she told us. "They are some more things from the letters you wrote, but these are positive in tone. That means they are favorable. In other words, they don't turn the reader off. They don't put the parent in a quarrelsome mood.

"You will notice some of these talk about shortcomings of parents, but there is a note of okayness. There is something to let them know they are all right. They haven't failed as parents."

Sure enough, these letters had a different feel from the ones we read yesterday:

Dear Stepmom:

I think you are really great! But there are a few things I think I should tell you that have been on my mind. Do you remember when I was in love? I tried to talk to you about what I felt, and you laughed. Mom, next time I want to tell you something, please don't ignore me or make fun of me.

127

Dear Mother:

The time has come for me to let you know what you have really done for me. At times you may think me a mess and ask yourself where you have failed. You haven't. I think of the times when I wanted to go somewhere or do something, and you said no. In the end, it was for the best most of the time.

Dear Parents:

Remember that I love you, and all my nasty remarks won't make me forget that. Of course, I have some complaints. I suppose all kids do. But when I'm old enough to move away from home, I'll miss you all. Dinner together Sunday afternoons. The card games. All the little things we take for granted seem more and more precious the older I get. Always remember I care. Even when I yell and scream at you I love you very much.

To my Mom and Dad—

We've always been close, and I've always felt I could go to you with any problems. That's why I feel hurt that lately I don't seem to be able to talk to you. It's as if you don't trust me. The point is, you are really good parents, and you have done a good job with us kids. So I think you could let us be more independent, and we wouldn't let you down.

Dear Mom and Dad:

Please don't look down on me for the things I don't mean to do. Forgive me with love, not punishment. I love you all the time even if the things I say and do seem to be the opposite. Sometimes my body takes over while my mind is sleeping. I would like to run to you sometimes and reach out for help, but I'm afraid you would be disappointed in me.

Dear Folks,

I hope you know I don't want to hurt either of you. Yet I feel our family is being torn apart. You work all the time, Mom, and I wonder if you are bored with the family. Dad, you go out a lot and drink. Sometimes I worry about maybe you are an alcoholic. I still love you as much as I always have, but I'm afraid we'll drift apart and soon be out of each other's reach. So let's be a family and laugh together once more.

So now I see what Mrs. Atkins is trying to tell us. I wonder if I should write a lovingly-yours letter to my folks. I wonder....

Something to Write to Parents

I did write a lovingly-yours letter. I think I would have even if it hadn't been an assignment. "Try to turn your complaints into pleas for a better relationship between you and your parents," Mrs. Atkins suggested. Some of us decided to give or send these letters to our parents.

Our class decided this assignment was a good idea. Maybe it's something you'd like to try. What do you think your parents' reactions would be? Do you suppose something you say in the letter might even have a lasting effect on the way your family gets along from now on?

37

Who, Me?

Mr. Dean stopped me in the hall on what we kids refer to as a "down-in-the-dumps day."

"What are you looking glum about *now*? he asked in an accusing tone. Mr. D. can read you just by looking.

"It's everything," I said. "The whole world. War going on everywhere. People starving. All that crooked stuff in Washington—"

"Beautiful or not, it's all the world we have," he interrupted.

"But—" I began.

"You aren't in India or Cambodia," he said. "By the way, have you volunteered some time at the Center for Children's Learning Disabilities?"

"Not lately," I said, wondering what the Center for Children's Learning Disabilities is.

"What are you doing about the new students at school?" he asked next.

"New students?"

He sighed. "The ones who enter during the school year, you know."

"Oh yeah, them," I said, standing there looking stupid.

He patted my shoulder. "This is your world, Kirk. Right here."

I looked at my watch. "Hey, it's about time for the bell. Be seein' ya." I grinned and waved and bounded off down the hall as if being on time to class was the most important thing on earth.

Somehow I knew what he was going to say next: "So what are you going to do about you?"

Topical Index